Edited by
STEVEN R. HIRSCH
JOHN HARRIS

Consent and the Incompetent Patient:
Ethics, Law, and Medicine

Proceedings of a meeting held at
The Royal Society of Medicine, 9 December 1986

GASKELL

ISBN 0 902241 22 2

Gaskell is an imprint of the Royal College of Psychiatrists,
17 Belgrave Square, London SW1

Distributed in North America
by American Psychiatric Press, Inc.

Acknowledgements
Publication of this volume was made possible by the generous
contributions of Upjohn UK Ltd, The Medical Protection Society,
The Medical Defence Union, and the Psychiatry Section of the
Royal Society of Medicine.

Typeset by Dobbie Typesetting Limited, Plymouth, Devon
Printed in Britain at the Alden Press, Oxford

Contents

List of Contributors

Sir Douglas Black, MD, FRCP, Royal College of Physicians, London

Mr Henry Brooke, QC, Fountain Court, Temple

Dr John Harris, BA, DPhil, Senior Lecturer in Philosophy, Department of Education and Research and Director of the Centre for Social Ethics and Policy, University of Manchester

Professor Steven Hirsch, MPhil, MD, FRCP, FRCPsych, Professor of Psychiatry, Charing Cross and Westminster Hospital

Professor Bryan Jennett, MD, FRCS, Professor of Neurosurgery, Dean of the Faculty of Medicine, University of Glasgow

Professor Elaine Murphy, FRCPsych, Professor of Psychogeriatrics, United Medical and Dental School of Guy's and St Thomas' Hospitals

Dr Richard Nicholson, MA, BM, BCh, DCH, Deputy Director, Institute of Medical Ethics, London (*closing final discussion*)

Sir Roger Ormrod, BA, BM, BCh, QC, PC, Kt, British Postgraduate Medical Federation, London (*opening discussion to Chapters 1 and 2*)

Mrs Dorothy Silberston, National Schizophrenia Fellowship, Surrey

Mr David Sullivan, QC, Harcourt Buildings, Temple

Mrs Shirley Turner, Chairman of the Mental Health Act Commission's Southern Region and Mental Handicap Group

Principal participants in the discussion (in order of appearance)

Dr David Greaves, Consultant Psychiatrist, Southampton

Dr Michael Raymond, Consultant Psychiatrist, Netherne Hospital and Sutton General Hospital

Professor Ian Kennedy, Department of Medical Law and Ethics, Kings College, London

Dr P. G. McGrath, retired Consultant Psychiatrist and past director of Broadmoor Hospital for the Criminally Insane

Dr Peter Rhode, Consultant Psychiatrist, St Mary Abbot's Hospital, London

Professor Sydney Brandon, Professor of Psychiatry, University of Leicester

Dr Pamela Taylor, Senior Lecturer in Forensic Psychiatry, Institute of Psychiatry and Honorary Consultant Psychiatrist, De Crespigny Park, London

Dr Thomas Bewley, Consultant Psychiatrist, Tooting Bec Hospital, *formerly* President, Royal College of Psychiatrists

Professor Gethin Morgan, Professor of Psychiatry, University of Bristol

Dr James Birley, Consultant Psychiatrist, and President, Royal College of Psychiatrists

Professor W. A. Frosh, Cornell University

Dr Pamela Mason, Principal Medical Officer, Department of Health and Social Security

Dr Gordon Langley, Consultant Psychogeriatrician, Member of the Mental Health Act Commission, Exe Vale Hospital, Devon

Dr Bernard Barnett, Member of the Mental Health Act Commission *formerly* Psychiatric Adviser to Children's Department, City of Birmingham Hospital

Mrs Teresa S. Myers, USA visitor

Dr R. N. Palmer, Member of the Secretariat, Medical Protection Society

Dr Seymour Spencer, Clinical Lecturer in Psychiatry, Oxford University

Dr John Bradley, Consultant Psychiatrist, Whittington and Royal Northern Hospitals, London, and Member of Council of the Medical Protection Society

Dr A. R. M. Freeman, Consultant Psychiatrist, Hillingdon Hospital and Secretary, Public Policy Committee of the Royal College of Psychiatrists

Introduction

STEVEN R. HIRSCH and
JOHN HARRIS

This book arises from widespread concern about individuals who are ill or handicapped in ways that render them incapable of making autonomous decisions about how they are to be treated. Such people cannot, of course, give valid or informed consent either to treatment or to their participation in research into their condition. Legally, they are described as lacking capacity, or mentally incompetent.

This concern has two dimensions. There is the concern that vulnerable individuals are protected from unwarranted treatment and research, and apprehension in some quarters that either of these might involve assault or battery on vulnerable individuals, and may be of only marginal benefit to the subjects. There is also the equally strong concern that vulnerable individuals receive the treatment that they need (whether they understand the need or not), that the best available care is afforded to them, and that research that may help such people be vigorously pursued.

It will be obvious at once that there is scope for conflict between these two, equally legitimate, concerns that we have about the treatment of vulnerable individuals. This conflict can, of course, arise in any area of health care, but most individuals, if properly advised, can strike the balance for themselves. It is where individuals are incapable of fully appreciating the nature of the decisions that need to be made about their care that the tension between these two dimensions of concern becomes acute. This book is, in part, an attempt to explore and resolve this tension.

However, the problem is acute for another reason, and that is the sheer scale of the problem. There are many thousands of such unfortunately incapable individuals in our hospitals, and at home, who cannot make decisions for themselves, many because they become suddenly too ill to make decisions for themselves, others because they are unconscious, and many more because they have long-term or permanent disability. Some will be a danger to themselves, prone to run away from those trying to help them, or unappreciative of the dangers posed by, say, electrical appliances, or other simple but potentially dangerous features of the environment. Such people may also in some circumstances constitute a danger to others, either intentionally or unwittingly.

Recent and urgent attention has been drawn to the problem of resolving the tensions we have referred to, by the publication of a document issued by the Mental Health Act Commission in 1985. This document, entitled *Consent to Treatment*, contained a draft code of practice governing the treatment of incapable patients and setting out their rights with respect to such treatment. The draft code of practice took as its point of departure an analysis of the law concerning assault and battery, which, it argued, if tested in the courts, would govern the practice of medicine and allied professions in the treatment of incapable patients. Having imposed these limits on their deliberations, the Mental Health Act Commissioners went on to outline when, and under what conditions, research may be done and when a patient may or may not be treated without consent.

The conclusions of the draft code of practice were broadly that patients who are incapable of consenting to treatment could not be included in any research that is not intended to be part of his or her treatment, thus ruling out so-called 'non-therapeutic research'. The Commission took the view that if its interpretation of the law were correct, there would be, in effect, a legal restraint against treating patients incapable of consent other than in ways specifically permitted by the Mental Health Acts, and against including them in non-therapeutic research. Leaving aside for the moment the question of the correctness of this interpretation of the law (this will be taken up in the first papers of this book) the draft code of practice was widely interpreted as advocating that the law of battery established the basis that governs the treatment of the incapable patient. The Mental Health Act Commissioners thus appeared to come down firmly on the side of interpreting society's responsibilities to incapable patients as primarily the obligation to protect them from violations of the person, and of giving this objective moral priority over claims that might be made about the value of such treatment to the patients themselves, to other sufferers, and to society at large.

Not unnaturally, this approach caused grave concern to psychiatrists and others who treat incapable patients and research the causes of such conditions as mental handicap, severe schizophrenia or mania, dementia, and the confusional delirious states of consciousness that can occur in these conditions and which seriously impair the brain's function. From this perspective, it appeared that the greater weight should be given to interpreting society's responsibility to such afflicted individuals along the lines of the second approach that we identified earlier, namely, in terms of ensuring that vulnerable patients receive the treatment that they need (whether they understand the need or not) and that the best available care is afforded to them even if they do not consent, and that research into their conditions is pursued.

The position is complicated by the fact that in research, there is no obvious alternative to using the patients themselves as subjects, as in most cases there is no adequate animal model. Research into the above conditions therefore cannot go ahead if those who cannot give consent are not involved. Concerned professionals fear that such patients and their successors will suffer as a result.

This, then, is the background against which this book is set. Our purpose has been to provide a balanced and comprehensive view of the issues involved in deciding what treatment and research is permissible on incapable patients.

This book is based on presentations and discussions held at The Royal Society of Medicine on 9 December 1986. There were 11 invited speakers and discussants, and 15 distinguished contributors to the discussions. We think this collection of papers and the recorded discussions explores deeply, and provides insight into, many important medico-legal and ethical questions regarding treatment and research for those unable to consent. The meeting was initiated, organised, and chaired in the morning by Professor Steven Hirsch, then president-elect of the Psychiatric Section of The Royal Society of Medicine, which sponsored the meeting, and chaired in the afternoon by Dr Leslie Dunn, president of the Psychiatric Section 1986–1987.

The first four chapters of the book correspond to the morning's proceedings and present the more theoretical and conceptual issues. They deal with how the law currently stands on these issues, and what judicial opinion is likely to be on such matters. Two eminent members of the Bar, David Sullivan QC and Henry Brooke QC, present the arguments regarding the extent to which the laws of battery and negligence are relevant, and Sir Roger Ormrod QC, Kt, a former Lord Justice of Appeal, opens the discussions. Then Sir Douglas Black expresses the deep concern of the medical profession and outlines the ways in which he sees the conceptual issues, and John Harris gives a philosophical analysis of the basis of the debate.

Chapters 5–8, corresponding to the afternoon's proceedings, deal with the practical consequences of different approaches to regulations as seen by a neurosurgeon, Professor Bryan Jennett, a psychogeriatrician, Professor Elaine Murphy, and two representatives of the wider public: Mrs Dorothy Silberston, who is a leading member of the National Schizophrenia Fellowship, an organisation for the relatives of patients; and Mrs Shirley Turner, who represents the Mental Health Act Commission and as it sees it, the public interest. Those who are less familiar with the issues from the patient's point of view may wish to turn to chapters 5–8 first. The final discussion is concluded by Dr Richard Nicholson, deputy director of the Institute of Medical Ethics.

One caveat needs to be entered. It is, of course, often extremely difficult to determine when, precisely, an individual is incapable of giving consent or, indeed, of making autonomous decisions generally. Equally, it is a matter of controversy as to what exactly is involved in autonomous decision-making. Both these problems, while real and important, are not our present concern. The contributors to this volume all concentrate on those people who are judged incapable of giving consent however problematic this judgement may be.

We hope that this book will help to clarify the issues and also contribute to a resolution of the debate and to the formulation of an improved code of practice, whether enshrined in legislation or adopted voluntarily by the professions. The range of issues considered here are, of course, of relevance far beyond the concerns of those dealing primarily with incapable patients and, we hope, will interest anyone concerned with society's responsibilities to its more vulnerable members who may, one day, include many of us. It will be of particular interest to lawyers, psychiatrists, health-care professionals, and members of ethical committees, as well as students of law, medicine, nursing, psychology, philosophy, and social work.

1 The incapable patient and the law

DAVID SULLIVAN

The two topics that I shall address are the law relating to the medical treatment of mentally incapable patients, and the law relating to the participation of such patients in projects of medical research. Let us be quite clear at the outset. These are topics with which the Courts have not yet had to deal specifically. Accordingly, one has to consider them in the light of existing legal principle, not of decided authority. The outcome of decisions on these issues is of fundamental importance. It will affect the treatment of thousands of patients residing in mental hospitals, such as those with dementia, severe psychosis, or severe mental handicap. Such patients have not been subjected to compulsory detention or, therefore, the provisions (both protective and enabling) of Part IV of the Mental Health Act 1983, relating to the treatment of detained patients, with or without their consent.

The context in which this debate arises is the conflict between two established principles of English law. I should emphasise that it is English law and not in any way American or other foreign laws, with which I am concerned. On the one hand, as the Divisional Court has said a short while ago in an analogous context: "The fundamental principle, plain and incontestable, is that every person's body is inviolate" (Collins *vs* Wilcock, 1984). To that principle, the law has already recognised a class of reasonable exceptions, to which I will return later. In its broadest form, this principle, the law of trespass to the person, simply embodies a very basic rule of ordinary human conduct: namely that, subject to obvious exceptions, you do not lay hands on another person without his or her consent. This principle is no bogey, even if it has been blessed with the emotive additional title of 'battery'.

On the other hand, there is the principle, also well established in English law, that the standard of care, to which doctors may reasonably be expected to attain in diagnosis and in treating patients with their consent, is the standard recognised as proper by any responsible and skilled body of medical opinion. In achieving any such standard, a doctor complies with his legal duty of care. Failing in it, he is negligent.

Each of these principles govern different aspects of the relationship between a doctor and his patient. There is no doubt that the law of trespass or battery is applicable to issues relating to treatment of a capable and conscious patient if no consent has been obtained from him at all. I mention this because it has been claimed that this principle of law has no application to any part of the doctor/patient relationship. If this claim was genuinely meant to apply to capable patients who had not given any consent at all, then I must reply that to my knowledge it is refuted by every relevant case that has been decided in law, every legal textbook, and every academic paper relating to the subject. Such a claim would not only affect the civil rights of the patient as a citizen, but would also, I believe, divert attention and sympathy away from the real interests of doctors. There are, indeed, genuine and powerful considerations that doctors can rightly advance about their legal position, particularly in relation to the problems involved in their treatment of incapable informal patients. It would be unfortunate if those considerations were prejudiced by a claim that doctors stand, uniquely, outside the well-established principle.

The right question, I would suggest, is whether the treatment of the incapable patient should be one of those areas (like the diagnosis and treatment of the consenting patient) where the law of trespass or battery does not apply. What are the exceptions already recognised or recognisable by the courts? The law tries principally to reflect the common sense of ordinary life. As one would expect, the law of trespass or battery does not apply to the inadvertent or other acceptable physical touchings of life; in the street, or between members of families or friends; to reasonable contacts in legitimate games; to a lawful arrest; and so on. All these are the obvious stuff of ordinary life. Another well-known and perhaps more relevant area where the normal rule about consent does not run is where an emergency arises; where an injured person has been rendered unconscious and urgently needs medical treatment to prevent his death or further injury. This is another of the obvious cases where any reasonable person would say "Of course, treat him as best you can, in such an emergency". A few years ago, all such examples were sensibly explained by a court as illustrations of what is "acceptable in the ordinary conduct of everyday life". It was the same divisional court that had enunciated the well-established principle, cited above, of the inviolability of the human body (Collins *vs* Wilcock, 1984). The Court of Appeal has also subsequently adopted that explanation, in dealing with a case of horseplay between schoolboys (Wilson *vs* Pringle, 1987). Although it is useful to have such a formula to embody such situations, there is nothing very novel in the reasoning behind it. It reflects both the common sense of the matter, and the way in which some of the earlier judges had explained their decisions in the individual cases before them.

With that kind of background, we come to consider the problem of incapable (informal) patients – those who are mentally incapable of giving a real consent to treatment. This is not, of course, to suggest that there are not many patients in mental hospitals who are quite capable of giving such consent. But the number of patients not so capable runs into many thousands. To my knowledge, there are no directly relevant legal cases or pronouncements, and scant discussion by writers, about these problems. We are in the realm of prediction as to what the courts will say, in the light of principle. We should not be misled into thinking that where there are no appropriate legal decisions to guide us, that there is no law – as laymen sometimes assume. The common law is certainly there, but it is unfortunately buried still 'in the breasts of the judges', as the phrase goes; to be extracted only by what surgeons might call an exploratory operation. My own view is that, given society as it is today, it is wrong that the legal position of doctors and of their incapable patients is not made clear, in the interests of them both. If it indeed be the will of society that doctors should always be able to dispense with the consent of incapable patients, let that be enshrined in some unequivocal form. If the contrary be preferred, then let that be enshrined. Alternatively, some balanced view, between those two extremes, could be worked out and accepted by society. However, at the present, we have these conflicting principles of law to reconcile.

At present only three arguments suggest themselves to me to support a contention that the principle of trespass or battery should not apply at all to the treatment of patients who are mentally incapable of giving a consent. First, it might be argued that, in principle, it is the more limited law of medical negligence (as summarised above) that should apply to the treatment of such patients. The grounds that might be advanced for such an argument are that only one set of legal rules should govern the whole of the relationship between a doctor and his patient. But we have already seen that such grounds cannot be valid, because a doctor is in any event subject to the law of trespass or battery, if he fails to get any kind of consent at all from a capable and conscious patient. However, support for such an argument might be sought in the recent House of Lords decision in Mrs Sidaway's case (Sidaway *vs* Bethlem Royal Hospital Governors, 1985). There, the judges extended the recognised 'medical standard' test for consenting patients from the field of diagnosis and treatment to the field of medical advice. However, the matter complained of was not a failure by the surgeon to seek and obtain consent from the patient, but the fact that he had not told her (as she alleged) of a material risk. The surgeon had in fact obtained the patient's consent in accordance with the requirements of the existing law, by telling her in broad terms what the nature and purpose of the treatment were. The judges, by a majority, have determined that a complaint about an omission to inform a patient of a material risk, when seeking his or her consent, has to be considered under the law of negligence. But when the matter which is at issue is the invasion (often long-term) of the body of an incapable patient, who has never given consent at all (and may actively be resistant to such treatment), the circumstances are quite different. It is also of interest in the Sidaway case that not only did Lord Scarman strongly dissent from the view that the standard of care (in relation to medical advice) should be no more than a standard acceptable in the medical profession, but even the majority of the judges held that the door should still be open for the courts, in particular cases, to hold that such a standard was not sufficient. This appears to be a pointer that the 'medical standard' test will not be extended without qualification to a new field, even when a treatment has only been given once, and still less so when an invasive treatment of a patient who is incapable of consent has to be sustained over a period of time.

Secondly, it might be argued that the treatment of an incapable patient without his consent should be regarded as something "acceptable in the ordinary conduct of everyday life"; and that within that particular pronouncement of the courts, the law of battery is not even relevant. But is the invasion of a patient's body without his consent and often against his physical resistance 'ordinary conduct'? Is it part of 'everyday life', in the way in which the courts have regarded physical contacts or emergency treatment? And to whom is it 'acceptable'? It is quite clear from any reading of their judgements that neither the divisional court (Collins *vs* Wilcock, 1984) nor the Court of Appeal (Wilson *vs* Pringle, 1986) were addressing themselves to mental-health situations, where medical treatment may involve frequent invasions of the bodies of patients who, while incapable of sufficient understanding to be able to give a real consent, may have very clear feelings towards the treatment proposed for them. Issues of mental-health treatments give rise to problems far beyond those of single events like the arrest of a suspect, an act of horseplay, or inadvertent or deliberate jostling in the street. In no legal case have the judges had to consider the implications of this specialised branch of medical treatment.

One other, a third, argument suggests itself to me. In the recent decision in the Court of Appeal (Wilson *vs* Pringle, 1986) (involving horseplay by schoolboys), the Court recorded that to constitute a trespass, a touching has to be a 'hostile' touching. But the Court went on to say that hostility was not to be equated with ill will or malevolence. Consider the case of an injection into the body of an incapable patient who resists it. How could it not be regarded as 'hostile' in that situation, judged by any test? Is it to be any different for a patient who does not resist but is passive? Is the distinction between the resistance or the passivity of a mentally disordered patient to govern whether the law of trespass should apply? Moreover I would suggest that the Court of Appeal's emphasis on the element of hostility as a necessary test is vitiated by the curious circularity of argument that may then become involved. Having ruled out ill will or malevolence as a necessary ingredient of 'hostility', the Court of Appeal then sought to explain the earlier decision of the divisional court (Collins *vs* Wilcock, 1984, relating to a temporary restraint by a policewoman), on the basis that the act there complained of was 'unlawful and in that way hostile'. But 'unlawfulness' was the very issue in the case; and the argument is therefore circular.

In my view, the courts could not and would not disavow the principle of the inviolable nature of the human body. Only if they were satisfied that sufficient measures were taken to protect the patient's interests within the limits imposed by his incapability, when balanced against the relevant professional problems and difficulties, would the courts regard the treatment as justified and an exception to that general principle. How much better, I would suggest, that people should face this problem in advance and that a common understanding be explored and reached as to what measures would be appropriate to satisfy society and the courts that everyone's interests were being protected – the interests both of the patient and of all the professions involved in such treatment. That, in my view, is the sensible way forward. It is also the way in which the Mental Health Act Commission sought in 1985 to address the problem in putting forward its proposals. Whether those proposals were right or not is clearly a matter for constructive debate. But in my view there can be little doubt about the principle of law, which forms the true background to such a debate.

[*paragraph added to original contribution at symposium*] I would conclude, on this issue, by adding that the recent decision in the House of Lords (*In re* B., 1987) about the sterilisation of a mentally handicapped minor, and the other recent decisions referred to in that case, do not appear to bear directly on the issue discussed here. But if they were thought to be material, they could be said to reflect the extreme concern with which both the Courts, and the wider public, regard the problems of giving what (on the particular facts of the House of Lords case) could be said to be 'treatment' to an incapable person.

I turn now to the related field of medical research, and the question of how the courts would regard such research if carried out on patients who cannot give their consent. Everything that I have said about the treatment of incapable patients applies, I suggest, even more strongly in relation to projects of research proposed to be carried out on such patients. No one doubts the need for medical science to be able to advance. To reconcile that need with the requirements of the law is, I believe, the essential task. In this field it is interesting that the paramount requirement of a patient's consent is present in every pronouncement of which I am aware, made by governments, institutions, doctors, and other professional bodies, since the last war, and indeed before it. I refer to the Nuremberg code of 1947; the Medical Research Council's statement of 1962; the Helsinki Declaration made in 1964 and revised again in 1975; the guide-lines of the British Psychological Society in 1983; the guide-lines of the Royal College of Physicians in 1984, and the recommendations made by the Institute of Medical Ethics as recently as September 1986.

In all these pronouncements, there is an unbroken thread of emphasis on the central issue of the need for consent. I suggest that this simply underlines a recognition of the principle behind the rule of law, both here in England, and in most of the world, that the human body is inviolable and that exceptions to it are only to be made under the rule of law. One has to ask whether such an exception would be allowed by the courts. Would it be permissible in law to carry out research on incapable patients who resisted? Would it be permissible on compliant patients? The onus in all cases would be a very heavy one. I would suggest that only under the most carefully thought-out and effective guide-lines might such projects be regarded as lawful by the courts. Otherwise, the projects would be illegal. The effective working of a full system of local ethics committees, proposed as long ago as 1967 and now in partial operation, would be one essential condition under which the courts might hold that invasive research procedures were, in particular cases, justified. The emphasis would undoubtedly be on the effective constitution and membership of such committees and on the guide-lines under which they should operate in relation to patients who cannot give their own consent.

It is clear that some members of the medical profession have had serious doubts about the operation of the present system; as is exemplified in pronouncements by the British Medical Association in 1985, and by the Institute of Medical Ethics in September 1986. These are welcome steps; but the essential problem remains the working out of satisfactory guide-lines in relation to incapable patients.

When considering what guide-lines in relation to research would be likely to gain full acceptance, it is essential, I believe, to start with what the Institute of Medical Ethics has recently said as a result of its survey of local ethics committees. I quote from its report:

> "There is too much variability in the structure and working methods of research ethics committees in England and Wales for one to have any confidence that they are all doing an efficient and effective job. . . .
> The evidence of the survey shows that some committees:
> – do not know to whom they are accountable;
> – are circumvented by some researchers;
> – either have no lay members, or lay members who are not independent of the health service;
> – have working practices that prevent them from fulfilling their function; and
> – may not understand the legal requirements for informed consent."

That is the point, I believe, at which any discussion of guide-lines, to reconcile the interests of the patient and the doctor, must begin. Progress from that point is in all our hands. The Commission has produced some thoughts about the issue. The debate is open; and the future lies, to a great extent, in the response of the medical and other professions engaged in this specialised branch of treatment and care.

To summarise this paper, I suggest that:
1. the courts would have to have regard to the principle of the law of trespass or battery, if they were called upon to consider the legality of invasive treatment of, or research upon, incapable patients

2. the courts have already accepted that some forms of ordinary conduct lie outside that principle

3. the task should be to establish the framework within which the treatment of incapable patients, and research in relation to them, can take place, on lines acceptable both to doctors and to the rest of society as the guardians of such patients

4. that task will only be advanced if the professionals respond by giving their views as to the guide-lines under which treatment of incapable patients, and research upon such patients, should be carried out; so enabling their views and the Commission's views and any other views to be debated. The ideal vehicle for a resulting framework would be the code of practice envisaged by the Mental Health Act

5. given an acceptable framework, the courts would be able to recognise that such treatments and research would constitute no infringement of the principle.

References

COLLINS *vs* WILCOCK (1984) 1 W. L. R., P. 1172; 3 All.E.R., P. 374
In re B. (a minor) (1987) 2 W.L.R. 1213 *The Times*, 1 May 1987
SIDAWAY *vs* BETHLEM ROYAL HOSPITAL GOVERNORS (1985) A.C. 871; 1 All.E.R., 642
WILSON *vs* PRINGLE (1987) Q.B. 237; 2 All.E.R., P. 440

Postscript

At this time, there is no full law report of the case of *In re* T., but a report in *The Times* (11 July 1987) indicates that the judge accepted arguments that the termination of pregnancy and sterilisation of a severely mentally handicapped woman (who could not consent) would be *prima facie* acts of trespass, and that such treatments were not within the category of 'exigencies of everyday life'. He interpreted Wilson *vs* Pringle in the light of Collins *vs* Wilcock (see above). This appears to vindicate the main thesis of this paper.

2 Consent to treatment or research: the incapable patient

HENRY BROOKE

I shall address the problem of the extent to which, in my view, the English courts will turn to the law of battery when they look for guidance as to the legal principles that they should apply in a particular class of cases. These are cases in which there is a dispute about the legality of the conduct of a doctor who in good conscience has treated, or conducted research on, a person who was incapable of giving consent to that treatment or research. I have been invited to assume that in treating the patient or in conducting his research, the doctor did whatever was normally expected of him by the standards of his profession; for example, he obtained, where necessary, the approval of the appropriate ethical committee, and he acted with due care. I will also assume, for simplicity, that the person who is unable to consent is an adult. I make this assumption because the common law has always regarded the parent of a child as a surrogate decision-maker who has, in an appropriate case, got the authority to make decisions for the child that are in the interests of the child. In the class of case that I am concerned with today, there will exist no surrogate decision-maker whose status as a person legally empowered to give any necessary consent is clearly recognised by English law.

I will first discuss the English law of battery. Battery is one example of what the common law calls trespass to the person, which is a type of activity infringing against the personal security or personal liberty of another that is condemned by the common law as a civil wrong and is actionable in damages when it takes place. Apart from battery, the other two civil wrongs that are categorised as trespass to the person are assault, which in simple terms means the threat of an unlawful battery, and false imprisonment, which means detention against a person's will for however short a period, in circumstances that cannot be justified by any rules developed by the common law or by statutory authority.

The traditional definition of a battery, which is set out in Halsbury's (1985) Laws, is an act that directly and either intentionally or negligently causes some physical contact with the person of another without that person's consent.

If he has consented to the contact, or if he has permitted it, expressly or impliedly, then there is no battery. However, in view of what I will say in a minute, I think it may now be better to redefine battery as being an act that directly and either intentionally or negligently causes some physical contact with the person of another in circumstances in which such contact is not generally acceptable in the ordinary conduct of life. The law of battery is not to be found in any act of Parliament. It has been developed by the common sense of English common-law judges over the centuries. When it is applied in the context of medical or surgical treatment, it is merely the law's expression of an elementary rule of a free society, which was expressed in clear terms by an American judge, Mr Justice Cardozo, over 70 years ago (Schloendorff *vs* Society of New York Hospital, 1914). This rule says that every human being of adult years and sound mind has a right to determine what shall be done with his or her own body. However, like all simple rules which are fashioned over time by the application of common sense, the rule admits of exceptions. Mr Justice Cardozo himself recognised in the judgement I have referred to, that the rule only applied in this absolute form to adults of sound mind. He also expressly excluded such adults from the application of the rule when they were unconscious and in need of emergency treatment. In those circumstances they would be in no condition to give consent. These limitations on the rule in the context of medical and surgical treatment are illustrations of the way in which the English common law has grafted limitations and exceptions onto the rule wherever it is sensible to do so, if the law is not to be an ass. For example, acts that would otherwise be unlawful batteries that are performed in reasonable self defence, or in the course of ejecting a trespasser from one's property, or in the exercise of parental or statutory authority, etc., have been treated as legitimate exceptions to the general rule.

In our law schools, we used to learn by rote a list of exceptions to the rule as if they were exceptions set out in a written code or in an act of Parliament. Earlier this year, however, the Court of Appeal rationalised all these different defences to complaints of unlawful battery, including the defence of consent. It has brought them all under the umbrella of a general exception which embraces all physical contact which is generally acceptable in the ordinary conduct of daily life (Wilson *vs* Pringle, 1986). In future, therefore, unless the House of Lords disapproves of this formulation of the defence, it will be a defence to a charge of an unlawful battery that in acting as he did, the defendant did something which was generally acceptable in the ordinary conduct of daily life. This will give the law much-needed flexibility, and a chance to develop, as accepted standards of conduct change.

In giving the judgement of the court, Lord Justice Croom-Johnson said that this rationalisation provided a solution to the old problem of identifying the legal rule that allows a casualty surgeon to perform an urgent operation on an unconscious patient who is brought into hospital. He said that hitherto it had been customary to say in such cases that consent would be implied for what would otherwise be a battery on the unconscious body. "It is better", he said, "simply to say that the surgeon's action is acceptable in the ordinary conduct of everyday life" and it is therefore not an unlawful battery. Although the same approach had already been adopted in a lower court by Lord Justice Robert Goff, who is now a Law Lord, in Collins *vs* Wilcock (1984), this judgement of the Court of Appeal was not available to the Mental Health Act Commissioners when they drew up and published their draft code of practice in the autumn of 1985 (Mental Health Act, 1983, Section 118, Draft Code of Practice). I believe that sections of Part IV of that draft code, which is concerned with questions of consent to treatment for the mentally disordered, would have been drafted differently if the judgement had been available.

The reason I say this is that at almost every turn in that part of the code, the authors seem to be advocating that those concerned with the care of the mentally ill should 'have their noses' in two different sets of rule books if they are to be sure that their treatment is lawful. Doctors and psychiatrists must not only know what are the standards of care of such patients that are accepted as proper by those who are expert in giving such care (which is the standard of care demanded by the law of negligence). The Commissioners also seem to be suggesting that they should be astute to follow more absolute rules when they are satisfying themselves about the extent to which their patient understands what is being proposed in the course of treatment, if they are not to be found guilty of an unlawful battery actionable in damages.

If this approach was well founded in English law, it would involve a reversal of the policy favoured over the centuries by English common-law judges that has permitted the caring professions to develop their own standards of professional care (which of course lay emphasis on the need to obtain the confidence and trust of patients) under the general coercive sanction of a professional-negligence action if the standards are not followed. If the Commissioners' repeated emphasis on the alleged requirements of the law of battery in their draft code is soundly founded in law, it appears to me to lead necessarily to the drafting of a set of regulations (as opposed to a set of guide-lines) for standards of professional care, which would have to be drafted by lawyers and civil servants, and not by doctors. I do not believe that such a change in the policy of English law is required by law. It must be for others who have far greater experience in these matters than I have to determine whether such a change, with its emphasis on the rule book and not on the doctor's discretion, would be in the best interests of the proper development of patient care.

In cases where there is no special difficulty arising from the patient's inability to understand what he is being told, the best legal statement of the demarcation between the areas of conduct by doctors and surgeons that are properly policed by the law of battery, and those areas that are properly policed by the law of negligence, is to be found in a recent judgement of the Chief Justice of Canada (Reibl *vs* Hughes, 1980). This judgement later set out the extent of the doctor's legal duty to inform the patient of the risks inherent in a proposed medical or surgical procedure in terms that are much more onerous than the English law of negligence is at present willing to recognise. But in the passage I am concerned with, the judge states very clearly that answers to questions that relate to the extent of a doctor's duty to inform a patient of the type of treatment that is proposed, are to be found by reference to the law of negligence, not to the law of battery.

The Chief Justice said that, in his opinion, actions of battery in respect of surgical or medical treatment should be confined to cases where surgery or treatment to which there had been no consent at all was performed or given, or where, emergency situations apart, surgery or treatment was performed and given beyond that to which there was consent. He continued in these terms:

> "I can appreciate the temptation to say that the genuineness of consent to medical treatment depends on proper disclosure of the risks which it entails but in my view unless there has been misrepresentation or fraud to secure consent to the treatment a failure to disclose the attendant risks, however serious, should go to negligence rather than to battery. Although such a failure relates to an informed choice of submitting to or refusing recommended and appropriate treatment it arises as the breach of an anterior duty of due care, comparable in legal obligation to the duty of due care in carrying out the particular treatment to which the patient has consented. It is not a test of the validity of the consent."

At this point, this judgement, in my opinion, correctly states the law that would be applied by English common-law judges. During the last 10 years, there have been efforts to introduce into English medical-negligence cases allegations that, although the patient signed a consent form, the doctor, or health authority by its servants or agents, performed an unlawful battery on him. It is said that the consent, although given, was not a valid consent because the patient did not really understand what was being proposed, or because the risks of the proposed treatment were not explained to him sufficiently clearly before he gave his consent.

Opinions have, of course, differed about the extent to which the doctor, in the exercise of the duty of care that he or she owes to his or her patient, should explain these things to him or her if he or she is to comply with the standard of care that is required of him or her. But every English judge who has considered the matter has robustly said that (apart from questions of fraud or misrepresentation), considerations about what a doctor ought to tell his patient, who has signed an apparently valid consent form, belong to the law of negligence, not to the law of battery. In the leading English case on the subject, the two members of the House of Lords, whose views were most diametrically opposed with respect to the extent of the doctor's legal duty to tell his patient about the risks of treatment, were united in holding that the solution to the problem was not to be found in the law of battery but in the law of negligence (Sidaway *vs* Governors of Bethlem Royal Hospital, 1985). Lord Scarman agreed with an English judge who had recently said (Hills *vs* Potter, 1984) that he deplored reliance on the torts of assault and battery in medical cases of this kind where the proper cause of action, if any, was negligence.

So far, I have been concerned with cases in which the patient has sufficient understanding to give what can reasonably be called a consent to a proposed course of treatment. In different areas of English law where questions of understanding have to be investigated – in a rape case, for example, where a question may arise whether a girl with a mental disorder can truly be said to have consented to the act of intercourse (Regina *vs* Long, 1975, *compare* Regina *vs* Morgan, 1970), or in a probate action where questions may arise about the capacity of the testator to understand what he was doing when he made the will that is under challenge (*In re* Beaney, 1978) – different levels of understanding may be required before a court may be satisfied that a consent was truly given or that a testator truly understood what he was doing. At one extreme, probate law demands a relatively high level of understanding when questions arise about the capacity to make a will. The criminal law, on the other hand, is content on the whole with a much lower level.

In the context of medical treatment of the mentally impaired and mentally ill, an American academic writer, Professor Goldstein, has justified an approach that is content with a fairly low level of understanding to what are called in American law determinations of incompetence, by pointing out that a finding of incompetence that deprives the patient of authority to decide for himself constitutes the ultimate disregard of his human dignity (cited by Glanville Williams, 1983). Professor Glanville Williams has suggested that such a patient should be held to consent if he knows that therapy is proposed after such customary details have been communicated as he is capable of grasping and does not object (Glanville Williams, 1983).

You may wonder why I have so far been concerned exclusively with patients who are, however dimly, capable of understanding what is being suggested, when the subject of my talk is the much more difficult question of the likely approach of common-law judges in cases in which the patient is incapable even of this small measure of understanding. I have adopted this approach in order to show that the future development of the law of battery and the future development of the law of professional negligence now seems to be running along parallel lines. In the law of battery, which on the whole is not concerned with questions which arise in the context of a caring relationship, such as a doctor–patient relationship, the courts are now willing to test whether physical contact with another human being is lawful by asking the question: did the physical contact constitute behaviour that is generally acceptable in the ordinary conduct of life? Similarly, in the law of negligence, the courts have refused, except in extreme cases, to impose standards devised by judges: instead they ask, did the standard of care adopted by the doctor on this occasion conform with a standard of care that would be accepted as proper by a responsible body of medical opinion?

In each case, the approach is flexible and is capable of adaptation to accommodate the differing standards of conduct that are regarded in different generations as acceptable and proper by those who are identified by society as being worthy of its trust in the difficult task of formulating, improving, and enforcing those standards. They will have expert knowledge of the wide ambit of discretion that a good doctor will need if he is to provide the best modern standards of patient care. They will also have knowledge of the contemporary demands that are made on doctors by an increasingly intelligent and concerned lay society. Provided that they do their job responsibly within the loose framework of law created by the common-law judges, the judges will not interfere.

It can therefore be seen that there is no need to invent new rules of the common law to accommodate the questions that we are discussing today. All that the common law will require is that what is proposed should accord with standards that are for the time being generally acceptable, and with the standards of proper care adopted for the time being by a responsible body of opinion in the relevant profession. If any question arose about the infraction of those standards, the common-law judges would also be likely to look at any guide-lines on good practice that might from time to time be published under the authority of Parliament. However, if the doctor's conduct complies with those standards and those guide-lines, it will not be stigmatised as unlawful. The job of setting and enforcing those standards ought to be carried on outside the law courts, and provided that the job is being done sensitively and efficiently, the courts will not intervene.

I turn therefore to the approach taken by the Mental Health Act Commissioners in their draft code. In 1983, Parliament brought into force for the first time an act that provided that no patient, of whatever category, might be given certain serious forms of treatment, such as psychosurgical operations on the brain tissue, unless he was capable of understanding the nature, purpose, and likely effects of the proposed treatment, and consented to it. In relation to the treatment of anyone who is suffering from mental disorder, whether a voluntary or a compulsory patient in a hospital or whether being treated in the community, this is the only specific statutory requirement imposed by Parliament in this new act over and above the requirements of the common law.

The act also set out in clear terms the circumstances in which most patients who are detained or who are liable to be detained under certain provisions of the Mental Health Act may be treated without their consent. The clear statement of what may and what may not lawfully be done to such a patient without his or her consent, which is in Part IV of the 1983 Act, ended the long debate about the extent to which those who had been compulsorily detained for treatment under the earlier act might also be compulsorily treated. With this category of patient, there is now no problem. However, as the Commissioners point out, in modern times, the power to order compulsory detention (which gives statutory authority for what might otherwise be challenged as a false imprisonment) carries with it a stigma, and there are today, they say, many thousands of patients who are incapable of consenting to treatment, but who are not detained compulsorily, and who in some cases are not detainable. For the treatment of this class of patient there are, as I have said, no new statutory rules.

Parliament has, however, to some extent filled the vacuum by giving the Secretary of State power to issue a code of practice that would provide guidance to registered medical practitioners and members of other professions in relation to the medical treatment of all such patients (Mental Health Act, 1983, s. 118). What this code should contain is now open to public debate. In my opinion, the quality of this public debate will not be enhanced by an overemphasis of the supposed requirements of the English law of battery, let alone the requirements of American law on these matters. I shall illustrate what I mean. The Commissioners' approach to the answer to these difficult questions was to start from what they say is the law that relates to cases of necessity (Mental Health Act, 1983, Section 118, Draft Code of Practice, para. 4.9.7). They say that the law relating to treatment without consent in cases of necessity has developed, for the most part, in the context of cases involving patients who have been temporarily deprived of their ability to consent, by physical unconsciousness. They say, too, that this branch of the law has not yet focused on the problem of the mentally disordered patient who is conscious but incapable of consent, but they suggest that limited principles similar to those applied in cases of necessity might be applied in the cases of such patients. The application of these principles would apparently involve a doctor having to allow such a patient's health to deteriorate until it reaches a point of no return, which is defined as a point at which, within a reasonable safety margin, the future threat to life or health cannot be stopped if treatment is not started.

It needs to be made very clear that the Commissioners are referring here to the development of American law in this field. They are not referring to English law, and the American common-law approach is different from ours. American society has been based from its earliest times on an explicit recognition of the importance of the liberty of the individual. This liberty is protected by the recognition by American law of certain fundamental individual rights, such as a right to give or withhold treatment for bodily invasions. If this is an enforceable legal right, then it is understandable that a system of law that is developed round such rights should strictly circumscribe the discretion that ought to be allowed to so-called 'agents of necessity' when they exercise an individual's rights for him or her, without consultation, in circumstances when he or she is unable to exercise those rights for him- or herself. The American common-law lawyer will therefore approach a problem of this kind by asking as a first question: 'What are the patient's rights?' Once the powerful effect of the patient's rights is known, he or she is bound to follow the Commissioners' restrictive approach to cases where the patient is incapable of exercising those rights for him- or herself. The English common-law lawyer, on the other hand, will acknowledge that acceptable standards of conduct demand that a person of adult years and sound mind should not have his or her body invaded without his or her consent, but does not talk the language of legally enforceable individual rights. Instead he or she would ask: 'Given that a mentally incapable patient has entrusted him- or herself, or that events beyond his or her control have entrusted him or her, to the care of a doctor in circumstances where he or she need not be compulsorily detained, what is the doctor's duty in caring for the patient and by what standards should it be judged?' This is a different question, and the difference is at the heart of the debate that is being conducted today.

A refinement is added to the debate, because the UK adheres to the European Convention of Human Rights, and any citizen of the UK now has a right of access to the European Commission of Human Rights, and, in an appropriate case, to the European Court of Human Rights at Strasbourg, if he or she wishes to complain that one of his or her rights that are recognised by the Convention is being infringed. Article 5 (1) of the Convention provides that everyone has the right to liberty and security of person. It follows that any guidance on proper practice must take into account this provision of the Convention. The Court at Strasbourg is developing its own jurisprudence and does not necessarily follow American case-law slavishly. Its existence, however, must certainly be taken into account in discussions of this kind. The difficulty is that it is not easy to foresee what view the European Court of Human Rights would take of the meaning of the right to security of person of a mentally disordered patient who is incapable of understanding.

At present, English judges need not take account of the Convention if there are provisions of English law, whether statutory or otherwise, that are unambiguous and binding on them. It may be that in due course the provisions of the European Convention will be made part of our own statute law, so that our judges would be bound to apply the Convention's provisions when they interpret English law, and there is certainly a respectable social, intellectual, and political case for English law to be reformed in this direction. However, this would involve a change in the law, and all that we need to notice at this stage is that any guidance must avoid including advice that clearly infringes any of the human rights that are recognised by the Convention.

Another challenge to the present condition of English law is made by those writers who condemn as paternalistic an approach to legal regulation in medical matters that is based on the phrase 'trust the doctor', and that does not acknowledge that patients ought to have legally recognised rights.

However, in the light of three recent decisions by the House of Lords (Whitehouse *vs* Jordan, 1981; Maynard *vs* West Midlands Regional Health Authority, 1984; Sidaway *vs* Governors of Royal Bethlem Hospital, 1985), nobody could successfully challenge the proposition that English law in this field is currently based on the proposition that doctors can be trusted. It is also based on the proposition that, subject to what I have said about the indirect effect of the European Convention, there are no legally enforceable individual rights (apart, of course, from rights created by statute) that the judges need to pay attention to in identifying the parameters of the doctor's duty.

For these reasons, it is in my opinion essential in the present debate to distinguish between three quite different questions. Firstly, except in those cases where Parliament has provided a statutory answer, as in Part IV of the Mental Health Act, 1983, what standards of care does the English common law demand when an adult patient is incapable him- or herself of giving a valid consent to treatment? Secondly, what should be the preferred method of identifying, publishing, maintaining, and improving those standards in the interests of patient care, in order to keep them in line with the demands of contemporary society? Thirdly (and very differently), is there anything to be said for reforming our own law by introducing into it principles of American law, whether derived from American case-law, or statute, as we search for appropriate solutions?

I have already suggested that the Commissioners ought not to have approached the answer to this problem by adopting propositions of American law without, at any rate, identifying their source. Of course, no harm can be done by introducing principles of American law into the debate, provided that it is made quite clear that this is being done and that English law is different. For instance, the concept of 'agency of necessity' is not used by English common-law lawyers. It will not be found in the English law books on the Law of Agency, and English common law has not in fact developed along the lines suggested by the Commissioners. There is therefore no need, as a matter of law, to adopt their rather drastic proposal that the patient should be allowed to deteriorate until he reaches the point of no return before something is done for him.

In a lecture he delivered in 1959, Lord Devlin said that the common law disliked the defence of necessity in whatever form it might be raised (Devlin, 1962). He suggested that if it was felt necessary to establish, in English common law, some special defence to a trespass claim in the context of a doctor–patient relationship, this defence should be based on the principle that a man who acts in the affairs of another for that other's benefit should be immune to an action of trespass if he showed first that there was a need for some action to be taken by someone, secondly that he took the action that his beneficiary must be expected to want done, and thirdly that it was impracticable to seek the consent of the beneficiary.

As I have said, the English common-law judges have not in fact gone down this narrow path Lord Devlin suggested a generation ago for identifying the legal principles that permit doctors in appropriate circumstances to treat their patients when they are incapable of consent. Instead, they have been content to leave the lawfulness of a doctor's conduct to be judged by contemporary standards of acceptable behaviour: what these standards demand will have to be worked out on a case-by-case basis. It may well be that the resolution of such cases will be assisted by the publication by responsible authorities, such as the Secretary of State, or the leaders of the relevant professional bodies, of authoritative guidance on what the observance of good standards of practice should demand. However, the question the judge will have to ask him- or herself is simply this: Was the doctor's conduct acceptable when judged by contemporary standards of conduct?

An illustration of the looseness of the English approach in contrast to the rigidity of the American approach can be derived from the treatment, by English law, of consents that are given by such a patient's next of kin. In the judgement to which I have referred (Wilson *vs* Pringle, 1986), Lord Justice Croom-Johnson said that the problem of the unconscious patient arose where the patient could not consent and where there might be no next-of-kin available to do it for him. There is, however, no principle of English law that I know of that states unequivocally that an adult patient's next of kin has the authority to take decisions about treatment on his or her behalf when he or she is incapable of taking the decision for him- or herself. It is, of course, clear from this dictum of a senior Appeal Court judge that he regarded it as too obvious to warrant explanation that a doctor who obtained consent for treatment from such a patient's next of kin and who otherwise conducted himself with proper care could not be held to have acted unlawfully in giving the treatment. He did not find it necessary to reach this conclusion by an analysis of legal rights and powers: he would probably say that he reached it by the application of common sense, which is what the English common law is all about.

The English approach, as I have said, regards the necessity for consent in circumstances where consent is possible, not as the means of enforcing an individual right, but simply as an example of conduct that is required by contemporary standards of acceptable behaviour. If consent is not possible, then it is not surprising that in English law there has never been seen to be any need for procedures for advance selection, or living wills, or durable powers of attorney, for health care or other American devices for the advance identification of surrogate decision-makers for a patient who believes that he or she is soon to lose the power to make decisions for him- or herself. English judges will merely test the lawfulness of what has been done by hearing evidence of what is regarded as acceptable practice in the particular circumstances of the individual case that is brought up for decision and by making findings of fact on the evidence that they have heard.

In contrast to this rather broad-brush approach, the American approach to the solution of questions like this runs along these lines: an adult patient has a legal right which entitles him or her to insist that nothing should be done to his or her body without his or her consent. Because this is a right recognised by the law, then so long as he or she is alive, there must exist some procedure sanctioned by the law for transferring the power to consent to a third party who may exercise the power when the patient cannot. All that will then be left will be a vacuum in those emergency cases that the patient has not provided for in advance, for example by making what is called, in some states, a living will. In those cases, when a patient's rights have to be overridden because an emergency has occurred in circumstances in which there is nobody who can lawfully exercise them, the doctor's power to do anything that is not immediately necessary to save life or health has to be very tightly prescribed and restricted so as to allow only what is absolutely necessary to preserve life or health and no more.

In my opinion, therefore, those who are responsible for developing and publishing guidance on good practice for the treatment of patients who are incapable of consent ought not to allow themselves to feel constrained by what they believe to be the relevant principles of American law, if they think that those principles are inappropriate in an English context. Nor need they feel themselves constrained by the supposed requirements of the law of battery. What I hope may emerge from this public debate is a set of guide-lines on good practice, that are published under the authority of the Secretary of State and that give recognition to the doctor's need for flexibility in the exercise of his clinical judgement, and that also take into account some of the concerns of contemporary lay society when the recognition of these concerns will not narrow the width of the doctor's discretion to the detriment of his patient. If such a consensus does not emerge, then I can envisage a day when a common-law judge might be given the invidious task of making a ruling on the issue of acceptable standards of conduct between rival contentions, published by different authorities who are in one way or another responsible for the care of patients, and this is an outcome that I believe that all who are concerned with the care of these patients would want to do their best to avoid.

I have said nothing so far about the approach of common-law judges in cases involving clinical research. This is a very much more difficult and controversial area, but what I have said shows the framework that, in my opinion, an English court would use to approach the issue in the event of any dispute about the legality of any particular course of conduct. Any code that might be published under the present statutory powers contained in Section 118 of the Mental Health Act cannot contain guidance on these issues, because Parliament has limited the scope of such a code to guidance on treatment and has not extended it to research. It seems to me on the other hand that there is a strong case for the publication of authoritative guidance on the appropriate procedures for determining what is acceptable and what is not. The reason I say this is that if there was a legal dispute in which a court were to find that clinical research involving an invasion of the body of an 'incapable patient' had taken place, in the present state of things it would be likely to inquire very carefully, not only into the authority that the doctor had obtained from any relevant ethical committee, but also as to the composition and working methods of the committee in question. The court might also think it important to know whether the committee had given its approval in accordance with the guidance given to it by any body that the court was willing to recognise as a source of responsible and authoritative guidance on issues of this degree of public importance.

This is an area of medical activity that is comparatively new to me. In order to help me to prepare this contribution, Professor Hirsch lent me a copy of a recently published book, *Medical Research with Children: Ethics, Law and Practice* (Nicholson, 1986) which contains the report of an Institute of Medical Ethics working group on the ethics of clinical-research investigations on children. Chapter 8 of this book contains a most interesting survey, of a type apparently never attempted before, of research ethics committees, and I am bound to say that the unevenness of the composition, practice, and procedures of these committees, which is revealed by this survey, would be likely to be of concern to a court. For instance, if a court heard that a controversial piece of research in this field had been sanctioned on paper by a small committee composed entirely of medical practitioners, and that good modern practice demanded that such committees should be larger and more broadly based, and that they should take their decisions on difficult issues at formal meetings, it would not necessarily hold that the activity was acceptable and lawful merely because an ethical committee had sanctioned it.

To sum up, I believe that the English common law allows a flexibility of approach to those who are concerned with the establishment of good modern standards of patient care. I also believe that there is nothing in English law, as I understand it, that should be construed as meaning that doctors are unable as a matter of law to continue to treat their mentally disordered patients in ways dictated by good standards of modern treatment merely because the patients are mentally incapable of giving consent to that treatment and there is nobody specially identified by English law as capable of giving consent on their behalf. So far as research that involves the invasion of the bodies of such patients are concerned, I believe that English common-law judges would be willing to adopt as guidance on good practice, the guidelines published by any responsible and authoritative body that they can see to be truly representative of the differing aspects of the public interest in this difficult field, and that they would not be deflected from determining what was acceptable by any dogmatic approach based on rigid rules derived from the supposed requirements of the law of battery.

References

DEVLIN, LORD (1962) *Samples of Lawmaking*, pp. 90–92. Oxford: Oxford University Press.
GLANVILLE WILLIAMS (1983) *Textbook of Criminal Law* (2nd edn). Stevens & Sons.

HALSBURY, LORD (1985) *Halsbury's Laws* (4th edn), vol. 45, para. 1311. London: Butterworths.
NICHOLSON, R. H., ed. (1986) *Medical Research with Children: Ethics, Law and Practice.* Oxford: Oxford University Press.

Cases cited

COLLINS *vs* WILCOCK (1984) 1 W.L.R. 1172.
HILLS *vs* POTTER (1984) 1 W.L.R. 641, Hirst, J.
In re BEANEY (1978) 1 W.L.R. 770.
MAYNARD *vs* WEST MIDLANDS REGIONAL HEALTH AUTHORITY (1984) 1 W.L.R. 634.
REGINA *vs* LONG (1975) 62 Cr Appr R 50 (*compare* Victorian case of Regina *vs* Morgan, below)
REGINA *vs* MORGAN (1970) V.R. 337.
REIBL *vs* HUGHES (1980) 114 D.L.R. (3d) 1 at p. 10.
SCHLOENDORFF *vs* SOCIETY OF NEW YORK HOSPITAL (1914) 103 N.E. 92 at pp. 93–94.
SIDAWAY *vs* GOVERNORS OF BETHLEM ROYAL HOSPITAL (1984) 2 W.L.R. 778 C.A. *per* Sir John Donaldson at p. 790.
IBID (1985) 2 A.C. 871; (1985) 1 All E.R. 643, H.L.
WHITEHOUSE *vs* JORDAN (1981) 1 W.L.R. 246.
WILSON *vs* PRINGLE (1987) Q.B. 237; (1986) 2 All E.R. 440.

1 & 2 Discussion

SIR ROGER ORMROD: We have had the great advantage of having two eminent lawyers put their cases adversarily in the most friendly way possible, and that is in the best traditions of the English Bar. These two papers discuss the law – legal rights, – they do not refer to ethical rights at all, and I think, in the context, they were right not to do so. But when it comes to talking about the law, each paper indulges in what amounts to an act of prophecy. They are trying to predict what the common-law judges will do in a situation that has never yet arisen, and the fact that it has never yet arisen is in itself highly significant.

So what do advocates do when asked to express views or advise about what the judges will do? It is great fun trying to make such predictions. First, it depends very much on the judge. But there are two things about this discussion which strike me. First, no one has said what they mean by 'incapable'. Until someone does this, it is not very helpful to argue about the law, because we all know that patients suffering from mental illness are variously incapable. They may misappreciate the situation. Their judgement is invalidated in one way or another. So talking generally about incapable people is, I think, dangerous. In the course of the discussion, this should be clarified.

The second point I should like to make is this. Why should anyone wish to bring in the law of battery to help us decide how we treat a mentally ill patient? To my mind it is an extraordinary proposition – and it has always been so – that the law of trespass has anything whatever to do with this situation. But it is only this year that the Court of Appeal has asserted this. The most recent case, referred to by both the speakers, is Wilson *vs* Pringle in the Court of Appeal, in which the Court of Appeal pointed out the fact, which has been obvious for years, that the law of trespass is about hostile behaviour. If you once accept that the law of trespass is concerned with hostile behaviour, you do not have to worry about complex collections of exceptions for this and that. To my mind it is retrogressive to go back to the law of trespass and/or battery in order to find legal guide-lines. I therefore think that Mr Brooke's approach is far preferable – that the English judges will always go from case to case, step-by-step, and they will avoid broad statements of principle, such as the universal principle of the inviolability of the human body. The latter is a good textbook-writer's general principle, but it does not help when you have to resolve a dispute in a court of law.

My suggestion would be that we are here engaged in an activity that repeats itself from time to time in medicine. Whenever there are difficulties over medical ethics, the instinctive reaction of the medical profession is to turn to the lawyers and ask the lawyers what the law is. The lawyers respond by trying to predict what they think the law will be, if it arises, although, in fact, it does not arise. So I think we are talking about an ethical issue. I quote something that Karl Popper wrote in 1945. He said this:

> "The responsibility for our ethical decisions is entirely ours and can be shifted on to no one else, neither to God, nor to nature, nor to society, nor to history. Whatever authority we may accept, it is we who accept it. We only deceive ourselves if we do not realise this simple point."

SIR DOUGLAS BLACK: I will touch on the point that Sir Roger made as to why we had not yet defined incapacity. One always remembers vividly the examination that one passes, and in the old days when membership of the Royal College of Physicians of London depended on writing an essay, I was invited, along with other candidates, to write an essay on testamentary capacity. It has been a puzzle to me how I passed that examination, but I think I know now, and it is because I talked not only about the mind, which is always very difficult to talk about, but also about the organic condition of aphasia, where the intentions of the mind for one reason or another cannot be made clear. As an organic physician I could write a lot more about aphasia than I could about the mind, and that is the explanation.

DR DAVID GREAVES: If I understand what is being said, I feel that the English common law is trying to develop a system of legal rules that is somewhere between a system of social rules and a system of moral rules. But it does so in a step-by-step process rather than by a more theoretical process.

If we come to the question of medical ethics, which I think is the key issue identified by our discussant; my view is that we have been looking in the wrong place all the time. We need to look philosophically at the nature of medical knowledge in a way that we have not been prepared to face hitherto as the lawyers have put this problem squarely in the hands of the medical profession. Until we do that I believe that we shall not get this question right.

PROFESSOR STEVEN HIRSCH: I wonder whether it is side-stepping Mr Sullivan's point to say that this is not the way the judges will interpret the law, rather than meeting the point squarely and saying what should not be the case. Lawyers do not talk about 'what should not' but 'what is not', and judges interpret the law as it stands. I think we are considering ethics when we decide what should be the principles and that should be a matter for the legislators.

MR DAVID SULLIVAN: I shall first respond to Sir Roger's remarks, i.e. to the points that he made as regards what the Court of Appeal has said in two recent cases. First, he referred quite rightly, as indeed I had anticipated in my remarks, to the Court of Appeal reference to the requirement that a touching to constitute trespass has to be regarded as hostile. You should know that the Court of Appeal made it absolutely clear in that case that 'hostile', as they were using it there, was not in any way to be equated with ill will – which is what one would normally associate with a concept of hostility – or any form of mal-evolence. You will remember I gave you the illustration. Suppose in the exercise of your duty of care for a patient you come to the conclusion that the patient, although incapable, requires an injection of drugs; and suppose also that the patient is resistant to that; how, I would ask, could the giving of the injection not be regarded as a hostile act, from the patient's point of view, assuming, as the Court of Appeal has said, that it is not to be equated with any form of ill will or malevolence?

Another point that Sir Roger made as regards the inviolability of the human body suggested that this concept was something that textbook-writers would use and that judges would not use. As I said to you in my remarks, that principle has been expressly stated by the Court of Appeal in another case two years ago, and I read just two sentences from the judgement of the then Lord Justice Goff (now Lord Goff):

"We are here concerned primarily with battery. The fundamental principle, plain and incontestable, is that every person's body is inviolate."

So I would suggest that the point Sir Roger made is one that has already received the blessing of the Court of Appeal. It is because of that attitude that I have advocated to you the likelihood that in the first instance the courts would regard the matter in the light of the principle of this law of battery; although, as I have said – and I think in this respect probably a great deal of what Mr Brooke and myself have said coincides – I think the courts undoubtedly would be favourably disposed towards regarding the treatment of incapable patients, provided it complied with certain guidelines and principles of treatment, as being a lawful exception to the fundamental principle that Lord Justice Goff referred to.

I would agree with Dr Greaves that one may come to the same conclusion as to what is the way forward after hearing either Mr Brooke or myself, whatever the principle of law involved is. It was because of that consideration that I said at the outset of my remarks that I was slightly dismayed to be set as adversary to Mr Brooke, as we should consider the steps that must be taken regardless of whether the law be the law of battery or the law of negligence. I echo Sir Roger's words that the courts regarded these matters as matters that ought to be dealt with outside the confines of courts and considered in the proper places, such as, for example, the debating halls of professional bodies, but I would suggest, also in the debating halls of other institutions in society that may be concerned to protect the interests of people other than doctors.

PROFESSOR HIRSCH: May I ask you one question, Mr Sullivan? How can the law uphold that the body is inviolate in an absolute sense and at the same time make exceptions to this principle? That is the crux of the issue.

MR SULLIVAN: The only answer I can give is that that is the way the law has developed. What is important about a principle is that the courts regard a practical situation that comes before them, and ask themselves whether – for reasons which have to be advanced to the court – an exception can be allowed to that principle. I cannot explain it other than to say that this is the way the common law has grown up. Common law is fragmentary and it grows as it goes along.

DR MICHAEL RAYMOND: If the word 'hostile' does not imply ill will or malevolence, what does it imply?

MR SULLIVAN: I hoped we would not get into the position of having to cite cases to you, but this is what the Court of Appeal said when trying to apply their test of hostility in the example of the police officer in Collins *vs* Wilcock.

"She touched the woman deliberately but without an intention to do more than restrain her temporarily. Nevertheless she was acting unlawfully and in that way was acting with hostility. She was acting contrary to the woman's legal right not to be physically restrained."

The question is, of course, whether or not the officer was acting contrary to the woman's legal right. If she was, it seems to me quite circular to consider whether the action was hostile; it was hostile because it was unlawful, and it was unlawful because it was in breach of the woman's legal right not to be physically restrained. So would I think not only that the principle of hostility is a curious one if it is not, as the courts have said, expressly to be equated with ill will and malevolence, but also, that in applying it they have used a completely circular argument.

PROFESSOR IAN KENNEDY: I think that anyone who looks to Wilson *vs* Pringle as the authority for anything – with the greatest respect to the Court of Appeal – will be disappointed. The circularity or the tautology of the argument is fairly clear. The court was looking for a word other than 'harmful' and they invented the word 'hostile'. I think that if one is in the business of prediction (and like good doctors, good lawyers should try to prevent their clients falling into the hands of whomsoever) that it is absolutely crackers to predict that a court will find a doctor liable in anything if he or she behaves responsibly in treating an incapable patient, however defined – and we can see from the Gillick case[1] that there **is** a definition. But what I am interested in asking Henry Brooke is this. If you say the court will inject into the law a rule that the doctor ought to follow acceptable practice, do you think the court will take as its guide the view of the medical profession unalloyed by the views of anyone else, or will the court say, as I would predict, that it must follow that which the medical profession deems is the appropriate standard of care, provided it 'gets it right'? This was the court's view in Sidaway *vs* Governors of Bethlem Royal Hospital (1984),[2] i.e. the court will reserve the ultimate capacity to discipline or some power to oversee the standard of care exercised by the profession.

MR HENRY BROOKE: Yes, I am sure that that is the court's approach. I am, however, worried that the medical profession might develop one rule of practice and that Parliament, and the Secretary of State with his code of practice, might develop another set of guide-lines, and the courts might, in a sense, be asked to choose between them. The court might decide to choose those guide-lines that took into account more carefully some of the worries and concerns of intelligent modern society that it felt the doctors' guide-lines had not taken into account. That is why I think that occasions like this, in which both sides of the debate are mirrored, are very important, as I can foresee trouble in the future if two rival sets of guide-lines emerge.

DR P. G. MCGRATH: The definition of battery is not totally irrelevant. It has been suggested that it should be extended to include detention. This is a matter which concerns every special-hospital doctor, because such doctors are enjoined by statute to care for people who are liable to be detained. In the execution of that duty we were taken as far as the European Court of Human Rights in Strasbourg on one occasion, and lost our case, because a responsible medical officer authorised the locking of a room door for what the patient and his advisers took to be an unconscionable period. In another case, like the policewoman mentioned above, a nurse put his hand

---

1. Gillick *vs* West Norfolk and Wisbech Area Health Authority (1986) A.C. 112; (1985) 3 All E.R. 402 H.L.
2. *op. cit.*, see p. 21.

on the shoulder of a patient to direct him and was taken to court. We lost that case in the court of first instance but the decision was reversed in the divisional court. How far does detention equate with battery?

PROFESSOR HIRSCH: I think we need to consider the central question which is that when patients are incapable of consent, can they participate in research if necessary, and be treated in an ordinary way, without very cumbersome regulations and rules? For example, the Mental Health Commission, in attempting to solve this problem, recommends that every time a prescription that involves a serious medical treatment is written, another consultant should be consulted about that prescription. That would be very cumbersome, but is an example of the attempts to 'get around' the question.

DR PETER RHODE: The first time I read the draft code of practice I found it difficult to fault in detail but felt profoundly uneasy about the general emphasis. My worry is that the issues are defined in terms of the law of battery and rather simplistically but David Sullivan emphasises that it is fundamental. The question of the exceptions is also oversimplified. I suggest that we as doctors operate on the basis of exceptions and our good practice is derived from the concept of consent. What we try to do for patients unable to consent is treat them in a least-different way from our patients who consent fully. I am therefore profoundly uneasy with the draft code of practice as it is at the moment. I think it should have much more emphasis on good practice, with footnotes about the law, emphasising that we generally operate in an area of exceptions to the law of battery.

PROFESSOR SYDNEY BRANDON: Doctors cannot but be impressed by the eloquence and measured terms with which lawyers consider the difficult problems that we face. I would agree that these are essentially unique and often very different problems. In debates, we often end up with two suggestions: one that we attempt to codify all the situations with which a doctor may be presented in order to make them more clear, and I suggest that that is impossible on the basis of the experience we have here, and another – made at a recent conference of philosophers and lawyers – that there would be a lawyer and a philosopher present in every circumstance because our decisions are clearly much too important to be taken by doctors. Surely we must eventually fall back on good faith and the duty of care, ensuring that our practices are not only up to the standards of the profession, but open to scrutiny by our colleagues and by the Commission and other groups. But let us not try to answer the questions that we cannot yet pose.

DR PAMELA TAYLOR: I feel there is always tension and confusion between lawyers and psychiatrists, in that we deal with problems from different viewpoints. I find it diffi-cult to accept the concept of the person being inviolate, as a sick patient has already been violated by disease. Perhaps we should be considering whether what the doctor does will increase or decrease that violation. I wonder if lawyers can help us with that issue.

PROFESSOR KENNEDY: I am not sure I follow that argument. We are talking about violations by human agencies, not microbes. With respect to Professor Hirsch's point – how do you deal with this apparently absolute and therefore accepted proposition – I would redefine it by saying it is a prima facie proposition, unless you can demonstrate it ought not to be accepted that you should not lay hands on people or touch them without their permission. But I think that when you have an incapable patient who is mentally ill, as defined by those with integrity – if the proposition that there is such a thing called mental illness is accepted – then I think you can take Henry Brooke's point and turn it round. The patient may have a right to be treated under those circumstances, if he or she is not able to ask for it, but is clearly in need of it. Then treatment is pursuant to the normal rules for treatment. As to who sets down the rules, I am not happy to leave it to Parliament but do not think it should be left to psychiatrists only, as doctors, like other professionals, sometimes want to do what should not be done, even out of the best of motives.

3 Guide-lines or gumption?
The role of medical responsibility: a view from the profession

DOUGLAS BLACK

Although we are not always aware of it, we doctors deal for the most part in probabilities rather than in certainties, whereas at the end of many legal roads there lies a clear-cut and inescapable 'yes or no' decision. Within that partial truth may lie the explanation for some of the disagreements about the draft code of practice which have arisen in the context of the Mental Health Act. Two questions seem to me to lie close to the heart of the matter:

What is the purpose and nature of *informed consent*? I believe it to be the process by which the patient can assess the risk of a medical or surgical treatment proposed and explained to him by a doctor, followed by his free agreement to it.

What, in this context, is *incapacity*? In relation to a rational judgement of the issues, it is a patient's inability either to form such a judgement (because of immaturity in minors, or mental illness or handicap), or to express it adequately (because of some form of aphasia).

My own profession is clearly divided on the value of guide-lines on the debatable ground where ethics, law, and medicine meet; my own position is, however, clear – I am opposed to sets of regulations, and not much in favour even of 'guide-lines'. My experience in the Joint Committee on Higher Medical Training over the years has shown me how easily a guide-line, conceived in the most helpful spirit of flexibility, emerges at birth as a monster of rigidity. And when a multidisciplinary team takes in hand the formation of guide-lines, the accretion of different insights builds up a mountain of obstruction both to therapy and research. It can, of course, be argued that these pragmatic criticisms apply only to bad guide-lines, which can then be rectified in consultation. But my worries go somewhat deeper than pragmatism, and have, I believe, a theoretical basis.

The difficulty is not in enunciating what look like sensible guide-lines on medical ethics – on the contrary, so many people are doing it that it must be fairly easy. Difficulty arises in two main ways: when guide-lines or maxims or rules or whatever are seen to be in conflict; or when it becomes clear that exceptions must be made to a guide-line that originally seems to be a categorical imperative. The relevant principles in our particular area can be stated as follows: 1. the patient's autonomy in relation to any procedure requires that he/she give valid consent; 2. the doctor (or other health professional) has a duty both of care and of confidentiality.

Conflict between the principles

When a competent adult patient declines to accept a treatment proposed by a doctor, even after adequate explanation, the principle based on autonomy must clearly prevail. The situation is more difficult when a patient, not competent for any of the reasons above, either refuses treatment, or cannot give 'valid consent' to it. (Here, I speak of 'valid' rather than 'informed' consent, to enable me to explore the situation when the patient cannot understand an explanation, or cannot give voice to his consent.) The form of explanation – oral, written, or certified by witnesses – is perhaps less important than evidence of the patient's understanding of it. Consultation with colleagues, an appeal to relatives or other suitable parties, can help the doctor, but probably does not make legally valid consent. In the case of therapy, at least with ordinary means of therapy, most doctors would probably give preference to their duty even over the perhaps doubtful autonomy of an 'incompetent' patient. The dilemma is greater in cases of research, since increase in knowledge is also of value. Any research on patients whose ability to give valid consent is in question has to be based on a balance of advantage, with the agreement of colleagues and of a properly constituted ethics committee. Therapeutic trials are in a way intermediate between therapy and research, and my own bias is much in their favour, provided they are properly designed.

Exceptions, other than those arising from conflict between the principles: the principle of informed consent

The main difficulty, well illustrated by the Siddaway case (Siddaway *vs* Bethlem Royal Hospital, 1984), is what constitutes 'adequate information'. Concealment of likely risks amounts to fraud; but to explain every risk, however trivial or remote, will induce patients to refuse treatment which would in fact be of benefit to them. I believe that Mrs Siddaway should have been compensated, but on a 'no-fault' basis; and I find it unedifying that she had to resort to the courts. Of course, if she could have foreseen the outcome of the operation, she would not have had it; but the surgeon, equally incapable of penetrating the future, would not have done it.

There is again a more difficult problem in research, that ethically requires disclosure of all risks other than any that would by common consent be considered negligible. Not that the concept of 'negligible risk' is easy, as it might include both a common but trivial risk, such as a mild headache, or the very remote possibility of a rather serious risk, such as is accepted by boarding a car, train, or aeroplane. In trying to explain risks either to patients or volunteers, it may be worth distinguishing between actual risk, if everything goes off normally, and potential risk, if there should be an untoward complication. Neither of these risks equates exactly with perceived risk, which tends to be less than actual risk in the case of employees and employers in industry, but greater than actual risk when the source of risk is new and unfamiliar.

The principle of confidential care

There are few if any situations that would justify withholding care, except insofar as committing resources to one objective entails inevitably the 'opportunity cost' of not having them available for some more important or cost-effective alternative. But there are important exceptions to confidentiality, some of which would probably be generally agreed, such as divulging health information that might lead to the prevention of terrorism or the detection of serious crime; and others that are much more debatable, such as the divulging of tax evasion or illegal immigration.

My case against 'guide-lines', if I may so phrase it, is thus based partly on practical considerations, and partly on a degree of theoretical suspicion, based essentially on my belief that the detailed circumstances of the particular case are paramount over general guide-lines. Perhaps my dilemma may be illustrated by the issues involved in the Gillick case. In this, there is clear and visible disagreement between the legal authorities themselves, and also between the British Medical Association and the General Medical Council. My own instinct might lead me in one direction in one family, and in another direction in another, as I prefer private judgement to reliance on authority, in company with Karl Popper, and also with Martin Luther, who said in a somewhat different context 'I can no other'.

In conclusion, and by way of an oblique summary, I would suggest that the privileged position that we occupy as members of a profession, medical or legal, as the case may be, is justified not only by our skills, but also, much more so, by the effectiveness with which we deploy them to protect our patients or clients. How well we do this may depend in part on how we look on our fellow members of the profession. If we think poorly of them, we will restrict them in a system of guide-lines. If we think well of them, we must educate them in the kind of issues we have been discussing, and then hope that they will rise to our expectations.

3 *Discussion*

PROFESSOR BRANDON: If, as I judge Sir Douglas's remarks and other previous comments, we are going to rely on the individual qualities of the doctor, his judgement and good faith, what steps should we as a profession be taking in connection with the selection and training of medical students and the training of our doctors?

PROFESSOR HIRSCH: I think that is a very important rhetorical question. But if we are to train, and embody principles in, the individual, we shall have created a new set of rules and guide-lines, so we are only taking the question one step backwards, with the difference that discretion and flexibility will be preserved for the doctor, if we want him to be able to exercise the former on behalf of the incapable patient.

I am concerned that while I have every confidence in my own personal ethical judgements and everyone here may have great confidence in theirs, I am not sure that I have confidence in your judgements or that you have confidence in mine in every instance. Therefore we do perhaps need some guide-lines. But more importantly, the barristers and judges are telling us that if we do not take the initiative then others will set the guide-lines for us. They may even create laws to impose their standards on us, which is one way of solving ethical problems. With all the difficulties in arriving at guide-lines, it may be better for us to try to find that common ground between the medical profession and the public view that can be generally accepted, rather than relying on individual decision-making.

DR THOMAS BEWLEY: I agree with you, because I remember an Irish judge once saying to me that he was always right about everything all the time, but not everybody saw it that way, and obviously everyone in this room agrees with his sentiments. But it seems to me that our discussion is about whether we play the game according to the rules or, as I would prefer, we play the rules according to the game. I would follow Sir Douglas Black on this. At the end of the day, I suspect that we all agree that we should not only treat patients, but also not do anything that will hinder proper research, the latter being a most difficult area. How do we carry out good research with people who are not able to give consent in a way generally acceptable in everyday life?

PROFESSOR HIRSCH: If the courts are to use the conduct of ordinary life as a principle, they might find it easier to accept that we should decide whether to give drugs, remove gangrenous legs, or operate on bed sores of patients who are demented, without their consent, than accept that we can decide to do trials of new medications or take skin biopsies for chromosome-counting in a certain type of very incapable mentally defective patient. It is not part of everyday life to take a skin biopsy, particularly if it is not part of the treatment itself, even if it were a minor injury for a great gain. These are hard questions, to which we have not yet faced up.

MR BROOKE: I should like to raise with Sir Douglas the thorny question regarding regulations or guide-lines. We live in a litigious age. I have been concerned in medico-legal matters for about 25 years now, and up to now the kind of issues that I have been concerned with, with one or two exceptions, are those that the medical profession has thought through. As such, in a court, in which of course lay society is making judgements, doctors who have been thinking about the matters in question for a long time can provide assistance. We are discussing very difficult issues today. There has been much more thought about them on the other side of the Atlantic. In assisting a court over the illegality or otherwise of an action, I wish to refer to a body that has clearly thought out the pros and cons of the particular form of treatment in question and can thus assist the court. One must consult guide-lines, or seek guidance. Otherwise the lay judge may make up the answer himself without the kind of help that he would appreciate from those who have thought about the matters.

SIR DOUGLAS: I would very much like to answer one or two of the points that have been raised. First, I would rescue Sydney Brandon's 'rhetorical' question, because I think that it represents the heart of the matter. Eventually, we rely on professional judgement, both legal and medical. I think that ventilation of these issues throughout the medical-training course, taking what guidance we can from ethicists, doctors, lawyers, people who have had experience of actual problems, is tremendously important. So I put proper training of doctors, both undergraduate and postgraduate, very much at the heart of this problem. We have not discussed these issues enough and I very much welcome the trend over the past 10 to 20 years or so to bring them to public debate and not solely professional debate.

Taking up Dr Bewley's point, a very important distinction arises, not from the character of the subject of whatever one is doing, but from the nature of the activity in which one is engaged. Providing therapy poses very different problems from those involved in carrying out investigative research. Therapeutically, your duty lies in giving patients what the 'man on the Clapham omnibus' would regard as reasonable information. If you give all the possible risks of all the worst outcomes, the only people who will submit to your operation are those who have been soundly reassured on the basis that that course of action is best for their health. In research, I think you have a duty to disclose all possible risks. In the end it is the volunteer who has to make up his mind whether the risk is acceptable. But it is perhaps worth drawing your attention to two categories of acceptable risk. It is a very difficult thing to define negligible risk, although many people have tried it. When I was on the Medical Service Council a few years ago, when carrying out X-rays on children for investigative purposes, we had to try to get a definition of a negligible risk, and the one that I suggested was the risk of moving from London to Aberdeen. That is an accepted risk, but it is nevertheless a real risk. But since it is generally accepted and people do not think about it, I thought it a reasonable attempt at a definition of a negligible risk.

Mr Brooke's point is a very important one. I think one does need guidance but I think it has to be consensus well-worked-out guidance, not necessarily encapsulated in too rigid a framework. I am certainly all for guidance arising out of discussion but I think some of the attempts at rigid guide-lines have not been satisfactory.

I take this opportunity to pay a great tribute to the legal profession in this country for not following the Americans in accepting negligence cases on contingency. It is always difficult when people have a financial motive, whether they are doctors or lawyers, although I am sure that in the case of the American lawyers it is usually a subconscious motive.

PROFESSOR ELAINE MURPHY: Could I put in a word for Mr Brooke and his guide-lines, because I think that professional groups do need guide-lines, as the sum of opinions that they can represent is more than can be evolved from individual people's consciences. Proper guide-lines, constantly updated by professional members, can be a real asset to us. However, although we are here today not to speak about the draft code of practice and *Consent to Treatment* documents specifically, there is a problem when guide-lines are imposed on our profession by a body, i.e. the Mental Health Commission, which we do not feel we own. If we are to have guide-lines, the profession themselves must feel that they are a part of their own consensus judgement.

PROFESSOR BRYAN JENNETT: I also should like to defend the principle of guide-lines. Guide-lines are useful, for example in deciding whether to withhold or withdraw treatment, as they have the advantage of being made away from the pressures of some particular crisis, and by a broader group of people than that involved in any individual case. It is important to note that they are guide-lines and not prescriptions. The art is in applying them, deciding whether or not – and this is what lawyers do with the law, I understand – they apply in a particular case. One has to remember the amount of critical medicine that is carried out by people of varying degrees of experience. There is nothing sinister about this, it is a fact of life. If one had Sir Douglas Black at your bedside, I am sure guide-lines would not be necessary, but it is a fact of life that many important decisions in urgent situations have to be undertaken by people of limited experience, for whom guide-lines are helpful, as they would also be to lawyers, I think.

PROFESSOR HIRSCH: I should like to ask Sir Douglas a question about a patient who is incapable of consent. If we wished to study diabetic coma, and felt it important to know something about the effect of, let us say, insulin treatment on the patient's glomerular filtration rate, but to ascertain this one had to inject a dye and measure its excretion in the urine, could we perform the research when the patient is incapable of consent if this action was regarded as having a very low risk?

SIR DOUGLAS: Common sense would say that you would, of course, do it. But if you have time, you first of all seek a proxy for the patient, e.g. a relative, and put the problem to them. If no relative or suitable person is available, I think you have to act as the patient's own proxy. Whether this is professional arrogance or not I do not know. The same sort of considerations apply to blood transfusions for children of Jehovah's Witnesses and so on.

To go backwards, Professor Jennett mentioned Mr Brooke's guide-lines, but I got the impression that the former was rather keener on guidance than on guide-lines. This may be wishful thinking on my part. Obviously I accept that it is a good thing to have discussion, and even to produce statements, but I think it is the rigidity of guide-lines and even more of regulations that worries me.

PROFESSOR GETHIN MORGAN: May I say something about recent dangerous trends in dealing with emergencies? In Bristol, we recently reviewed the clinical care of overdose patients and unearthed some terrible dilemmas, such as ambulance men who visit an individual's home and have to wait until the person becomes unconscious before they can transport him to hospital because they fear they will be subject subsequently to litigation for assault; the sister in casualty who has to allow a patient to walk out through the door, even though he or she may have taken a massive overdose of toxic drug; and the house physician who is unable to give an antidote because the patient refuses, and appears to be conscious and perfectly *compos mentis*. These are terrible dilemmas and people are becoming defensive in the practice of medicine because they fear litigation. I hope that matters will change so that staff who have to deal with problems such as these will feel able to act decisively in the interests of patients without undue fear of adverse repercussions. It is particularly important that junior staff should be able to consult senior colleagues without delay, should they need to do so.

PROFESSOR HIRSCH: I would like someone seriously to consider the matter of research. Let us consider the patient in whom we wanted to inject a dye to measure kidney function. This would not be part of his particular therapeutic treatment, but would be for the development of knowledge about the effects of the use of insulin in patients in diabetic coma. This course of action would not benefit that patient, but could be important for treatment in the future. Could we go ahead then?

SIR DOUGLAS: I think again it is a matter of checks and balances, if I may speak like an American. It depends to some extent on a trade-off between three things. First is the importance of the question that is being asked. I think trivial or unscientific research is to some extent unethical, if not as much so as is cruel research. Second, what is the actual trauma that you are inflicting. This has to be weighed against the potential benefit. Third, can you find someone, e.g. a relative, who would take the burden off your shoulders to some extent. I realise that is not legal consent, but you cannot get legal consent from a patient in a diabetic coma, and I feel marginally more comfortable if I have talked with relatives and explained to them, first, the purpose of the research, and second, what the experiment would mean in terms of risk and discomfort. The question of discomfort does not usually arise with an unconscious patient, but there can be delayed discomfort if you inject in the wrong place, for example.

PROFESSOR HIRSCH: I think you have clarified what probably is the general medical practice and attitude in these matters, but this attitude has been challenged. Starting with Mr Sullivan's proposition of inviolability of the body, one moves to the position where no third person can consent to another person being battered, and therefore it can be argued – and I think was argued effectively in the Commission's document – that although we may feel it is all right to go ahead in the circumstances we are discussing, there is no legal basis even if the risk is small and the relatives consent. But I sympathise with your point.

4 Professional responsibility and consent to treatment

JOHN HARRIS

The problems created by the tension between a professional's obligations to his or her clients or patients on the one hand, and the requirement that the patient or client should autonomously consent to any treatment on the other, are particularly profound in relation to psychiatric services (Harris, 1985). I propose to treat the question of the professional's ethical responsibilities to his patients or clients and the question of the moral constraints upon the discharge of those responsibilities as general ones, not as issues for medicine alone.

I suppose it would be agreed (at least until the fine print was read) that the practices both of medicine and of law are subject to review by higher authority, i.e. morality. Neither health professionals nor lawyers should do what is morally wrong. Just as wicked laws should neither be enacted nor enforced, so also doctors and other health professionals should neither violate nor ignore moral principles.

Problems remain both as to which moral principles apply and how they are to be interpreted. While we may be sure that just as a good ground for objecting to a law is that it is unjust, and to a medical procedure that it harms the patient, so the problem of how to apply our moral principles in what lawyers call hard cases is likely to remain acute. For example, consider the cases we are discussing, where violating the will of a mental patient in order, say, to discover more about his condition, involves a conflict of principles. One approach to this problem of how to understand our moral responsibilities to others where our principles seem to conflict we owe to the philosopher Ludwig Wittgenstein.

Understanding our concepts

Wittgenstein showed us that in order to understand the meaning of a concept, we need to do more than analyse the terms of the definition or reflect upon paradigm cases in which we would want to employ the concept. We need principally to understand the **point** of the concept. This involves reflection upon just why we are interested in the idea at all, and in understanding the particular value we attach to the classification it effects.

To take a medically neutral example, during the Vietnam War, protestors in the USA burnt the American flag, and in some cases their 'draft cards', as ways of expressing their opposition to the prosecution of the war. Some of them were charged, I think, with treason or at any rate with disrespect for the Flag (something akin to treason in the USA). They defended themselves by arguing that their action was protected by the First Amendment to the Constitution of the USA (which guarantees free speech). The Supreme Court eventually accepted the idea that in the circumstances, the flag-burning constituted an eloquent form of expression and that as such was protected by the First Amendment (Ely, 1975).[1] The point of this story is to show that simple reflection on the meaning of 'free' and 'speech' and on the paradigm cases of their use in conjunction with one another, will not help in considering whether or not the actions of the protestors in cases like these amounted to a form of 'speech'. But consideration of the **point** of the First Amendment, of protecting the freedom of speech of citizens, enabled the court to see that the reason for this protection was to secure for citizens freedom of **expression**, and that to confine 'expression' strictly to the spoken or written word would, in Ronald Dworkin's words, miss 'the point of the connection between expression and dignity. A man cannot express himself freely when he cannot match his rhetoric to his outrage, or when he must trim his sails to protect values he counts as nothing next to those he is trying to vindicate' (Dworkin, 1977, p. 201).

Now it seems that one way to interpret the dilemmas and anxieties that have occasioned this volume provides striking parallels with the cases before the United States Supreme Court. For just as in those cases a strict conception of the meaning of 'speech' confronted the protestors' felt need to express themselves, so here a strict understanding of what the common law means by 'assault' and 'battery', confronts the medical practitioner's view of what he or she is really doing to and for his or her patients when he or she lays hands upon them in circumstances in which they are incapable of giving consent.

Perhaps then we should ask: what is the point of a code of practice governing the treatment of people in the area of mental health? Why do we take an interest in mental health at all, and why do we bother to formulate codes of practice to govern our treatment of such patients? I suggest (although I do not think there are any conclusive arguments) that the point of this code of practice is to embody the idea of *respect for persons*, and to see that this idea is the

---

1. The two principal cases cited by Ely are: Spence *vs* Washington (1975) 418 US 405 (concerning flag desecration), and US *vs* O'Brien (1968) 391 US 367 (concerning draft-card burning). I have paraphrased these cases freely.

one which informs and regulates our treatment of those, including incapable patients, over whose lives and health we have power. Now perhaps this is going too far ahead. Surely the code of practice is supposed to provide rules of conduct consistent with the requirements of the Mental Health Act, 1983 and to protect the rights and interests of those affected by that act. Of course this is true, but contrary to popular belief even in academic circles, rights and interests do not appear fully fledged in our midst. They are part of an attitude of benevolent concern for others, and of course for ourselves, and are inexplicable except against a background of such concern. The ethic which best expresses this concern in a form usable as a principle of conduct, is *respect for persons*. It is this idea, having at its centre the idea of equality (Dworkin, 1977, p. 192), that I believe best explains and clarifies the ideas at issue today. To see why this is so we must for a moment look more closely at the idea of respect for persons.

Respect for persons

The attitude to others that we call 'respect for persons' has at its centre a principle of equality just because it expresses the idea that it is persons who are valuable – morally important – and hence that each is valuable in virtue of the things that make him or her a person (Harris, 1985, ch. 1) and hence that each person is as valuable as any other. And so to each must be shown the same concern and respect as is shown to any. But what exactly is involved in showing respect for all persons equally? I want to suggest that there are two essential dimensions to this attitude to others we call respect for persons. They are essential in the sense that no one could coherently claim to respect others if their behaviour failed to exhibit both dimensions. Someone who has respect for persons will then show both: 1. concern for their welfare; and 2. respect for their wishes. Normally these two dimensions of respect for persons are complementary, but there are many cases where there is some tension between them, and it is at these points that some of the most acute dilemmas of medical ethics occur.

Concern for the welfare of others

When health-care professionals accept that their first duty is to act always in the best interests of their patients, they are acknowledging the welfare dimension of respect for persons. Welfare is not, of course, here used as a technical term – it means what it usually means, 'the state or condition of doing or being well' which includes things like happiness, health, and living standards.

The reason that respect for persons cannot consist solely in concern for their welfare or in acting in what we believe to be their best interests, is that these attitudes to others are compatible with both paternalism and moralism. Briefly, *paternalism* is the belief that it can be right to order the lives of others for their own good irrespective of their own wishes or judgements. *Moralism* on the other hand is a comparable belief that has, at its centre, concern not for the welfare of others but for their moral character. The moralist believes that it can be right to order the lives of others so that 'morality' may be preserved.

Both the paternalist and the moralist are genuinely concerned for the welfare of others. They argue that it cannot be in your interests nor can it be conducive to your general welfare if you either do what is not good for you or act immorally. Despite the genuineness of this moral concern, both paternalism and moralism involve treating the agent as an incompetent. They deny the individual control over his or her own life and moral destiny and treat him as incapable to run his own life as he chooses. While both involve genuine concern for the welfare of others, neither can lay claim to demonstrating respect for their wishes and priorities.

Respect for the wishes of others

Respect for the wishes of others is central to any claim to accept that the lives of others matter. For each individual life has unique value and that value is determined by the way in which an individual shapes her own existence, choosing what she will do and how she will live. Because it is we ourselves who give value to our own existence, we need freedom to pursue our own objects in our own way. Unless the value of our lives is to be undermined, the only constraint upon our freedom to do as we please would be the familiar proviso, made famous by John Stuart Mill, that what we please to do does not harm others or does as little harm to them as it is possible for us to do.

Mill had another argument to offer for the freedom of the individual to pursue his own plans for his life. I am inclined to connect this freedom with the value of life itself, but Mill connects it with a person's capacity to improve himself and with the improvement of humankind.

> "He who lets the world or his own portion of it, choose his plan of life for him, has no need of any other faculty than the ape-like one of imitation. He who chooses his plan for himself employs all his faculties. He must use observation to see, reasoning and judgement to foresee,

activity to gather materials for decision, discrimination to decide, and when he has decided, firmness and self control to hold to his deliberate decision. And these qualities he requires and exercises exactly in proportion as the part of his conduct which he determines according to his own judgement and feelings is a large one.
It is possible that he might be guided in some good path and kept out of harm's way, without any of these things. But what will be his comparative worth as a human being?'' (Mill, 1972, p. 198)

The problem for all who care about others is how to reconcile respect for the free choices of others with real concern for their welfare when their choices appear to be self-destructive or self-harming.

One sort of comprehensive self-harming preference with which we are concerned today is that exhibited by a refusal to consent to treatment that would be beneficial, or by an inability to consent.

One classic way out of this dilemma has been for those who care about people with self-harming preferences to argue either that the self-harming preference is not a genuine preference, or else that it is not genuinely autonomous and therefore is not **really** what the individual wants.

This is not the place for a comprehensive account of autonomy. However, the *Draft Code of Practice* is surely right when it indicates (4.4.4–4.4.8, p. 71) that an individual's capacity to make autonomous decisions is unlikely to be comprehensive at any level and relates to the complexity of the particular decision and the information necessary to make it, so that an individual may be capable of autonomously deciding whether or not to undergo one treatment but not another. Those who drafted the code of practice are also correct to claim that even those who are detained under the Mental Health Act are not necessarily incompetent to give consent and that it is consequently always necessary to see in particular cases and with respect to particular decisions whether this is so (4.4.4 and 4.4.5, p. 71).

In this way they are following John Stuart Mill who warned in the most forceful terms against enlarging the class of individuals deemed unfit to make their own decisions. Lawyers should perhaps be forewarned that the following passage taken from a footnote to Mill's essay *On Liberty* may be offensive to those of a sensitive disposition.

''There is something both contemptible and frightful in the sort of evidence which, of late years any person can be declared judicially unfit for the management of his affairs; . . . All the minute details of his daily life are pried into and whatever is found which, seen through the medium of the perceiving and describing faculties of the lowest of the low, bears an appearance unlike absolute commonplace, is laid before the jury as evidence of insanity and often with success; the jurors being little if at all less vulgar and ignorant than the witnesses; while the judges, with that extraordinary want of knowledge of human nature and life which continually astonishes us in English lawyers often help to mislead them'' (Mill, 1972, footnote p. 198).

So, although one cannot hope to show respect for persons unless one has both concern for their welfare and respect for their wishes, it does not follow that both dimensions of respect for persons are of equal importance. Mill is surely right when he claims that an individual would be a poor sort of human being if his capacity to make something distinctively his own out of his life by the exercise of his own preferences were not respected; and that respect for wishes must have priority where the two dimensions of respect for persons conflict.

That said and while the danger that Mill and the Mental Health Act Commissioners point to, of unjustifiably enlarging the class of persons deemed incapable, is a real one, the question that remains is: What should health professionals do when faced with patients who are incapable of giving consent and who need help?

To answer this question we need to think again of the point of our concern and reflect on the circumstances which might make too legalistic an understanding of the principles involved simply self-defeating.

The obligation not to injure

The obligation not to injure other people is clearly entailed by the obligation to show respect for persons and arises from both dimensions of that obligation. It is now a commonplace (Harris, 1985, ch. 2) that we can injure others as much by our decisions not to help them as we can by positive assaults. That the law fails fully to recognise this is, of course, irrelevant. Anyone involved in health care knows that in the management of a patient's condition, professionals make innumerable decisions both to make interventions of various kinds and also to refrain from so doing. Each of these can be crucial and all affect what happens to the patient. So a technical and literal 'laying on of hands' is irrelevant to the issue of whether or not what the professional has done has harmed the patient.

If a patient is capable of consenting to treatment and wants to be helped, a professional who deliberately refrains from giving, say, a life-saving drug is as culpable as one who gives a death-dealing overdose. If the patient is not capable of consenting and has not indicated his preferences at a time when he was so capable, then again, if he needs medical help either to save his life, restore his general health, or put him once again in a position to be able to decide for himself, then the professional would be injuring that patient if he fails to do what is required for these ends. And of course this is so whether what is required is positive action – laying on of hands – or negative action – masterful (or not so masterful) inactivity.

The parallel with education

There is perhaps an important parallel here with the morality of our treatment of children with respect to education. To fail to educate an individual capable of achieving autonomy with the help of education, is to deprive that individual of the ability to choose between competing conceptions of a life worth living or of the worth of trying to live. It is to prevent or delay that individual's acquiring the ability to give his or her life its own particular character and value. This is comparable to failing to treat a debilitating but curable disease and both cases would be failures in our obligation not to injure other people. Conceived in this way, the limits on our right to treat in the absence of real consent are easy to determine. The point of autonomy, the point of choosing between competing conceptions of the good life, is simply that it is only thus that our lives become in any real sense our own. The value of our lives is the value that we give to them. And we do this as far as it is possible at all, by shaping our lives for ourselves. Our own choices, decisions, and preferences, however crude or simple, disastrous, or inappropriate, help to make us who we are; for each helps us to confirm or modify our own character and develop our ability to understand ourselves.

Paternalism ceases to be legitimate at the 'point of transition' at which it, so far from being productive of autonomy, frustrates the individual's own attempts to create his own life for himself. And this is true however crude, rudimentary, and capable-of-improvement those attempts may be. The point of transition occurs just when the paternalist interference does not operate to **enable** the individual to make choices or hasten his ability so to do, but operates to frustrate the exercise of choices, which are part of the individual's attempts to pursue his own conception of how to live. And again, this will be true however alien to ourselves and however crude when compared with our similar attempts, this individual's choices may seem. I do not suppose that this point of transition is easy to determine. However, even the theoretical mapping of this point does tell us something about the constraints on professionals with respect to their treatment of patients, and we are now in a position to draw some conclusions. Before doing so, however, we must consider whether or not the practices used in research in any way parallel those used in treatment.

Research

Whereas it can be claimed that to fail to treat a patient with an established therapy is to do that patient an injury, the same claim cannot straightforwardly be made as to the obligation to undertake research. Of course, so long as there is a reasonable chance of the research culminating in advances in therapeutic techniques, or even for that matter in advances in knowledge, there may be an obligation to undertake it, for to fail to do so will arguably damage society, and present and future individuals. However, a problem obviously arises where the research must be undertaken on present individuals for the sake not of improvements in their health and welfare, but of advances that will only be of advantage to others. Where individuals are capable of consenting to such research being done on themselves, and where such research is unlikely to be risky or injurious, they clearly ought to consent. And if they do, whether or not such research is risky or injurious, there is no problem. For an autonomous individual can freely consent to run risks or undergo injury if he or she so chooses. But if the individual is incapable of giving consent or it is doubtful whether a valid consent can be obtained from them, may they be made the subjects of research?

Where, as will often be the case, there is negligible risk to the subject and no pain, discomfort, or indignity involved in the research, and where the research is otherwise soundly based, both ethically and scientifically, then, surely, it would be wrong to fail to undertake worthwhile and beneficial research simply because the subjects of that research are incapable of giving an informed consent. The reasons for this may be illustrated by the following. Suppose there is a major accident as a result of which the lives of many thousands of people are in imminent peril. To rescue them we must place a few others at some small risk to themselves and subject them to some discomfort or anxiety. This might happen for example where the captain of a cargo vessel diverts into a storm to go to the rescue of a stricken passenger liner. The captain subjects his crew and the few passengers he is carrying to some risk and anxiety in order to save the thousands on the stricken liner. He would be culpable if he said: 'I cannot help the liner because that would involve some (minimal) involuntary risk to my passengers and crew'. There can be no absolute right to live a risk- and anxiety-free life at the expense of the lives of others.

We have a similar problem with, for example, people who disagree with private motor transport or nuclear power stations or other dangerous establishments or practices, and feel they are subjected to involuntary danger and risk for the sake of some greater good or social advantage, as they perceive. The point here is that the balancing exercise is a familiar one and does not involve a radical departure of principle. The same principles apply to scientific and medical research.

If there is a real expectation of substantial benefit from research and the risks are minimal and the research involves no pain, discomfort, anxiety, or indignity, then it should be undertaken, and those capable of consenting should consent. The fact that some subjects are incapable of consenting makes no difference to the legitimacy of the research.

Now it may appear that this principle goes much too far. For the analogy with the shipwreck seems to indicate that wherever there is palpable benefit from a course of action, and small risk and so on involved, then people are not only free to pursue that course of action, but are positively obliged so to do. This is not the case. The analogy shows merely that there can be no absolute principle that entitles individuals to live free of all involuntary imposition of risk. One important difference is that whereas those on the stricken ship are in real and present danger, those who will benefit from research are future and speculative. Because the advantage to be gained is future and speculative, we are entitled to demand that risks imposed for such gains be genuinely negligible and that the discomfort, anxiety, and indignity of any research procedures be truly minimal.

Where this is the case, all reasonable people should consent to such procedures. But what if they do not? Because the benefits are speculative, it is doubtful whether except *in extremis*, it could be justifiable to proceed with such research against the wishes or without the consent of research subjects. And of course if it is true that reasonable people would volunteer, then we can expect them to do so in sufficient numbers for there to be no need for any involuntary or non-voluntary research to be carried on. I say except *in extremis* because there can be cases where although the benefits of research are future and speculative, the danger is so profound that research is of the highest priority. AIDS might be such a case.

Now what of those who cannot consent? Here again the principle that people should not be the subjects of research that will not benefit themselves is clearly inadequate. If the research can only be done on those incapable of consenting and if it is sound and likely to be beneficial and involves minimal risk, discomfort, and so on, then clearly it should be done. To fail to do it would be to abandon voluntarily those present and future individuals who could benefit from the research.

Because this conclusion is controversial it is especially important to be clear about what is meant. This is not the place for an exhaustive account of just what it is that makes research sound from both an ethical and a scientific point of view. However, clearly the research must be into a problem the solution of which will benefit humankind. It must be undertaken by competent individuals who have a reasonable prospect of success and whose research protocols have been well worked out and have been submitted to a competent ethical committee. Moreover the research must be such that it is incapable of being undertaken without using subjects who are unable to consent and where there is no significant risk to those subjects.

Of course, it will be asked, who is to say what risks are significant or for that matter what procedures are undignified or involve discomfort or pain? But the answer is simple; all rational people are capable of making such judgements. What we must ensure is that panels (ethical committees perhaps), of impartial persons approve each research proposal and assess it in the terms we have set out.

Conclusions

Because it is the centrality of respect 'for the wishes or preferences of individuals into the ethic of respect' for persons, it is essential that all individuals capable of consenting to particular treatments or courses of management within health care, give real consent. The corollary is that real refusal to treatment should be respected even where it is self-harming or self-destructive.

However, conceding the importance of respecting the wishes of patients capable of giving real consent, health professionals are surely right to insist that when they touch incapable patients in order to help them, it is consistent neither with the common law nor with our concern to protect citizens with mental-health problems, that such behaviour be thought of in terms of assault and battery. This is because where patients are incapable of giving consent, then the obligation we have not to injure other people requires that they be given beneficial health care, whether that treatment is required to restore or improve their general health, remove discomfort, or restore or improve their capacity for autonomy. The present state of the law in which it is doubtful whether incapable patients can be treated for physical illness except in cases where serious deterioration or death will result, is clearly a nonsense. The common law here, so far from protecting the individual citizen from gratuitous injury, seems positively to encourage the infliction of such injury. This leads to the third conclusion.

The common-law offence of battery or assault is far too crude an instrument to rely on in working out a code of practice, which should be based on and sensitive to, the ethical principles that bear upon the treatment of patients in the area of mental health. A code of practice should start from ethical principles relevant to health care, not from common law, which may serve quite different interests. There is a general point here of considerable importance. It is that just as the Warnock Committee misconceived its task and undermined its moral authority when it limited itself to following public opinion rather than attempting to lead and direct it, so the Mental Health Act Commissioners missed the same sort of opportunity when they elected to follow the common law rather than to work out what the law should be and to recommend a code of practice that embodied such a view. One might ask, in the case of both the Warnock Committee and that of the Mental Health Act Commissioners: What is the point of assembling the great and the good to deliberate on public issues if all they are going to do is follow, in the one case popular sentiment, and in the other principles of law many hundreds of years old?

When we consider the special case of research rather than that of treatment, the same principles apply. It is in everyone's interests, including those who may be incapable of consent, that research is permitted to proceed, even where that research is (probably) not for the benefit of the subject of the research. Where such research involves no danger to the subject or minimal danger, and the research is likely to be beneficial, i.e. not frivolous or unnecessarily repetitive or simply curious, then it is in everyone's interests that it proceed. If such research can only be done on patients incapable of consenting and it is calculated and likely to be beneficial for other such patients or even for other patients in the future, then a reasonable person and a just and ethical society must consider whether the technical battery to present patients is not less of an evil than injury to the future beneficiaries of the research.

References

DWORKIN, R. (1977) *Taking Rights Seriously* p. 201. London: Duckworth.
ELY, J. H. (1975) Flag desecration: a case study in the roles of categorization and balancing in First Amendment analysis. *Harvard Law Review*, **88**, 1482–1508.
HARRIS, J. (1985) *The Value of Life: an Introduction to Medical Ethics*. London: Routledge and Kegan Paul.
MILL, J. S. (1972) On liberty. In *Utilitarianism* (ed. M. Warnock) p. 198. London: Fontana.

4 Discussion

DR JAMES BIRLEY: I welcome Dr Harris's views, which make sense to the average psychiatrist. I particularly welcome the Wittgensteinian approach of looking at the respect and dignity of the person, and the undignified idea that a person who is incapable should be automatically assumed to be unwilling to take part in research. I think that the Mental Health Commission have accepted Mill's view that to regard incapable people as requiring the protection of some sort of section of the Mental Health Act would be a degrading affair. Therefore we are in the dilemma of making, I think, ethical rather than legal judgements about them, although I do not have a solution.

On another point – and recalling earlier mention of quotations from Karl Popper's *The Open Society and its Enemies* – one has to say that at least until fairly recently, the average psychiatric hospital has not been a particularly open society. In the old days, at least, all the letters were answered by the superintendent. There was ample scope for idiosyncratic behaviour on a scale that caused alarm and scandal. So I think the issue of how one protects incapable people from such behaviour is still an issue that perhaps applies more to psychiatry than to other branches of medicine.

PROFESSOR W. A. FROSH: I should like first to comment on the problems just raised, relating to idiosyncratic behaviour. Some of the developments in the USA grew out of a series of quite horrifying experiments, many of them, although not all, done by government facilities, using psychiatric and mentally retarded patients without appropriate controls. The issue is not only about how to educate physicians, as was questioned this morning, so that they can behave appropriately, but how to maintain standards throughout years of practice. Again I think the issue of recurrent observation of standards of practice is a difficult one that certainly has not been resolved in the USA.

I share the speaker's reservations about guide-lines although they may indeed be the way to make the rules yourself and have others follow them. However, there has certainly been an increase in the influence of guide-lines in the USA. What starts out as a guide-line becomes a rule interpreted by the courts, or a guide-line that is not quite clear is clarified and eventually becomes a set of regulations to which one is held if a case comes to court.

In our discussion, we have considered 'easy' examples: patients with physical illness or with coma. What about the depressive patient who says 'I don't want tricyclics' and who may be a suicidal risk, or the schizophrenic patient who is delusional and refuses appropriate phenothiazine? Are they competent or not? I think most of the ordinary practice of psychiatry deals with the grey areas, not with those incompetent patients whom our common sense may be adequate to handle, but with those whose degree of competence in any particular instance is difficult to establish.[1] Of course, we must then ask: what is competence? When you get informed consent, what does it really mean? In the USA we have had a whole series of studies of this. In a study carried out by a colleague of mine, research subjects had to reach a certain criterion in an examination on the information used in the study before their signed consent to participation was accepted. All subjects reached this criterion, but it was subsequently found that their supposedly informed consent was not based on consideration of the real risks/benefits ratio, but was a measure of the relationship of the subject with the person seeking his or her consent. Many years ago I was doing a pharmacological study on schizophrenic patients. I was concerned that we might not be carrying out efficient testing of the efficacy of a drug if, after the informed-consent procedures, we were losing, as a result of their presumably being less likely to consent to participation, a greater percentage of paranoid patients compared with others. We decided that we would do an initial clinical screening for every patient who came in, and then we would compare the preliminary ordinary clinical data of those who refused and those who accepted. As it happened, I had a marvellous research assistant and nobody refused. It was very simple. This rather charming woman would sit down with the subject, and talk until she had developed a relationship, and every single one of the 100 patients who were approached for the study signed an informed consent. I wonder how informed that really was.

DR PAMELA MASON: I wish to add a historical dimension, following the comments of the last speaker, to which I think we have all responded positively. Prior to the enactment of mental-health legislation, we considered the whole issue of consent to treatment (I shall not comment about consent to research). It seemed that we should take the law on battery as the starting point, and then identify exceptions. Those that were made were for detained patients. These patients were legally held for clearly defined treatment of their own particular mental disorder only, and their exception to the law of battery was nothing to do with their incompetence to consent to treatment. We then looked at appropriate safeguards. As such, we limited the field as debate in Parliament requested. There are procedures in English legislation to override patients' refusal or incapacity to consent, for their own good, and these procedures have worked well in practice. At this time in question, however, it became apparent that there was great public-debate pressure to clarify the law further, but eventually the limits of the law as it existed were applied, I think quite rightly. We are raising similar points again now. Two earlier contributors felt that the law of battery guided us so far and no further; and that having made explicit some clear exceptions for consent-to-treatment procedures, we are now focusing on other areas that were not clarified in this mental-health legislation, i.e. treatment for physical disorders for the incapacitated patients. During the passage of the legislation I referred to above, the idea of the code of practice developed, because, I think as Dr Harris said, the law is quite a crude instrument when you are looking at clinical practice. It was felt that a code of practice could be drawn up that would be a consensus of professional opinion and public opinion, and that this would help us avoid American-style law practices where judges and lawyers consider only whether doctors have broken the law, and not whether they have adhered to guide-lines. Thus, the code of practice must have

1. Editors' note: The 1983 Mental Health Act states that a patient may be confined to hospital and also under what conditions the patient may be treated against his or her will and how his or her competence to decide on accepting or rejecting treatment should be determined.

a very firm basis in acceptance and understanding, and perhaps should not pursue the 'law-of-battery line', but be based on guide-lines or guidance, on clinical matters and practice, and on ethical matters. Finally, Lord Justice Ormrod's comment that, when we turn to the law on getting into ethical difficulties, we find the law does not serve us well, strikes me as very pertinent.

MR SULLIVAN: I entirely agree with the earlier part of Dr Harris's argument, but in his conclusions I think (as an immediate reaction) that he has totally missed the effect of English law in his analysis. He concludes that the Commission has endorsed the inviolability principle – which has certainly been enunciated by the judges – without any regard at all to the exceptions that the law has recognised, and I am sure will continue to recognise, quite clearly. Dr Harris suggests that what the Commission put forward as suggestions for a code of practice was that incapable patients could not be treated without the law being broken. It was the function of the Commission simply to make suggestions to the Secretary of State, who would then consult and eventually produce a code of practice. As I hope you appreciate, I was advocating the view that the courts would recognise quite clearly an exception to the principle of the inviolability of the human body and would do so undoubtedly willingly in relation to incapable patients, while maintaining certain requirements to ensure that the interests of all were being adequately protected. If the professions, lawyers, and society generally do not between them develop such guide-lines, and I use the word advisedly in spite of what Douglas Black has said, then I have little doubt that a court hearing that invasion of the human body had taken place without any form of protection of the interests, certainly of the patient, but also of society, might well decide at the end of the day that an exception had not been established. The way forward under English law, as I see it, is to establish clearly a common consensus for the method of treating these people. The question is not, as Dr Harris has said, whether or not the doctor should treat such patients, nor is it a question as to whether or not a failure to treat would constitute battery. The right consideration, I would suggest, is under what kind of conditions these patients should be treated. That is the way out of the legal principle as to what constitutes an exception that I was enunciating this morning.

DR JOHN HARRIS: I was exercising a rare luxury in acting in utter disregard of the law, because the legal question I considered was that of what the law should be. I set out what I thought were the moral principles that best explained, not particular decisions of judges, but the area of concern that we have for other people (in which the law of battery also operates). I feel that the principle of inviolability of the person must, for it to have any purpose, be understood in terms of what is required to show respect for the person. This respect may be regarded as one dimension of our benevolent concern for others. This is not very helpful in dealing with the incapable patient, because by failing to treat somebody and thereby worsening his or her condition, one injures him or her quite as effectively as when one batters him or her, and in these sort of cases more effectively. I think this is in agreement with what Ian Kennedy has said in terms of rights, although I do not use his language.

PROFESSOR HIRSCH: Are we really saying now that to trespass on another person's body is to offend under the law of battery, but to fail to do so as a doctor, for example, when you have a duty of care, is to be guilty by the law of negligence? If that is the case, surely some kind of clarification needs to be made.

MR SULLIVAN: I entirely agree with what Dr Harris and the Chairman have just said. Dr Harris concluded, whether wittingly or unwittingly, that in some way or other the code of practice was suggesting that doctors should fail to treat these patients. That is not so. The question, as I said a moment ago, is not whether they should or should not treat these patients – obviously they should – but under what conditions?

PROFESSOR HIRSCH: I think that is true. We were misleading those of you who have not read the code of practice carefully. The code did try to deal with the exceptions and to provide guidance for what to do about the people who needed treatment but who would apparently be battered if we did treat them. But many of the medical profession are concerned that the guide-lines became so explicit and difficult that they paralysed freedom of action for doctors to act as they thought best in the patients' interest – this is what Sir Douglas Black emphasised.

DR GORDON LANGLEY: I should like to underline what David Sullivan said. The Working Party was aware of the law of battery, but there was no wish to impose it to the detriment of a patient. Certainly, as a psychogeriatrician, I could never have gone along with that. The importance of balancing issues was stressed constantly throughout the code-of-practice document, although the duty of care was possibly given less emphasis than the problem of the law of battery. I feel we have three main problems, of increasing difficulty, with the obtaining of real consent as we have defined it. The first is to give patients a certain amount of broad-term information, which we have discussed. The second is in dealing with an action for negligence when some harm has come to the patient. Thirdly, the most difficult problem is with the North American standard of informed consent. Viewed as one large problem, the difficulties surrounding the real-consent issue may seem insurmountable, but if we divide the problem into a series of smaller issues, we may make progress more easily than some of the earlier contributors have suggested.

DR BERNARD BARNETT: I thank Dr Harris for referring to mental-health professionals, not just doctors. I think the designers of the code of practice considered carefully the number of professionals in the average mental-health team, the way responsibility was handled in relation to detained patients, and the whole business of interdisciplinary teamwork. As such, within any one discipline, there might be objections to the code of practice's being a multidisciplinary document, and perhaps the difficult aim of compiling such a document was not fulfilled.

SIR DOUGLAS: I always like, towards the end of a debate, to establish some common ground and I should suggest something along these lines. As members of professions we enjoy tremendous privileges. These are based not so much on our skills as on the way in which we deploy them to protect patients or clients, depending on whether we are doctors or lawyers. There are probably many ways in which we can do this, but we could polarise them into two extremes. We can either expect the worst of our professional colleagues, in which case we impose comprehensive guide-lines, or we can expect the best of them and are then obliged to take a deep interest in training, exemplifying, and having public discussion about them. It is my optimistic hope that if you expect much of people in professions they will rise to your expectations.

DR HARRIS: I would like to mention one thing in connection with informed or real consent, and particularly to take up what Professor Frosh was saying. We should not try to measure whether individuals have actually given an informed consent.

We should apply the standard of the electoral process, where no knowledge of the issues or indeed even the names of the candidates is required in order to cast a vote, because people are entitled to disregard the information they are given if they want to. We should measure informed consent in terms of the level of information given and whether it is appropriate to the person it is given to, not in terms of what that person's actual understanding is. We may be interested in that latter question just to test the adequacy of the information, but I think that we should not think that someone has given an unreal consent if he or she has chosen voluntarily to disregard the issue and has just said 'OK, go ahead'. That is his or her prerogative.

PROFESSOR HIRSCH: I fear we have only begun the debate, and we shall have to concentrate more on the research issues. In practice, clinicians do not have too much difficulty in taking effective action when they feel the need to do so. But the situation for research is, I think, more doubtful, because there are large numbers of patients who could be deprived of the benefits of research. If their own lives are not at stake, then the lives of those similarly afflicted in the future will be, if medical knowledge does not advance. But can medical knowledge advance in the context of the legal and ethical issues and principles that have been raised so far in this debate?

5 Medical implications

BRYAN JENNETT

My task is to consider the implications for medicine as a whole of the code of practice proposed by the Mental Health Commission when consent for treatment, or for participation in research, is required from an incompetent patient. The Commission's draft proposals seem to make it clear that it intends its recommendations to be all-embracing – not just for detained patients, not just for hospital patients, and presumably not just for psychiatric patients. If that really is the intention, then the repercussions could be felt in many specialties in medicine. This is because in the non-psychiatric wards of the country's acute-case hospitals there are probably many more patients incompetent to give consent than there are in psychiatric units – and there are a whole lot more in the long-stay geriatric wards.

Specialisation in medicine now results not infrequently in dilemmas of this kind, because there are many patients whose problems are not confined to the interests or expertise of one medical discipline. For example, there are more elderly patients admitted to surgical wards than to all acute-case medical and geriatric units combined. Yet it is geriatricians who are often turned to for policy advice about the old. In the case of incapacity to give consent, it seems that we might have to cope with proposals for which the only medical advice taken was from psychiatrists. I am unconvinced that the resulting recommendations take sufficient account of the different kinds of non-psychiatric patients who cannot give informed consent, or of the variety of circumstances in which consent may need to be sought.

In acute-case medicine, there is more concern with ethical imperatives than with legal constraints. I am uncertain whether those involved with the present proposals appreciate how much activity there now is in the field of medical ethics. I speak as a member of the governing body of the Institute of Medical Ethics and a member of the Nuffield Committee on the Teaching of Ethics to Medical Students. The principles of beneficence, non-maleficence and patient autonomy, together with that of allocative justice, are the central issues. In the USA, there are now no less than 70 professors of bioethics, and in many hospitals there are ethics grand rounds. In some there are ethicists carrying bleeps waiting to be called to the bedside for ethical emergencies. Psychiatrists do not feature much in this field of activity on either side of the Atlantic. However, several cases have been taken to court in the USA in attempts to have decisions about treatment or non-treatment made in a legal forum. In most states, however, the judges indicated clearly that they believed that this was the business of doctors. Nor did they seek to make detailed recommendations about the framework within which they should do this. They did, however, emphasise that it was the patient's welfare and his own presumed wishes, not the views of his relatives, that were paramount – should these appear to differ.

My task is to indicate the extent to which these matters are now a daily concern in acute-case medicine in Britain. Whether or not it is useful or practical to have detailed recommendations that span all the problems that can arise in such different circumstances as acute-case medicine and psychiatry is a matter that I shall leave for discussion, once I have described some of the dilemmas that could arise.

Incompetence in non-psychiatric patients

The range of patients not competent to give consent in acute-case hospitals includes three main groups. These are minors (from neonates to those in their early teens) who may need intensive care, dialysis, or unpleasant drugs for cancer. Then there are the elderly with varying degrees of organic dementia who may require surgery or other forms of rescue therapy for physical conditions unrelated to their antecedent dementia. Lastly there are adults of sound mind who are suffering impaired consciousness that is the result of critical illness that requires urgent treatment. Such conditions include head injury, intracranial haemorrhage and other forms of stroke, meningitis and encephalitis, failure of liver or kidney function, and consequences of drug overdose, whether accidental, therapeutic, or self-administered.

Until a decade ago it was commonly assumed that patients could readily be classified as conscious or unconscious. We now recognise various levels of coma as well as other disorders of consciousness. We know that when all the cells of the grey matter of the cerebral cortex have been wiped out the patient can survive for a decade or more in what is now called the vegetative state (Jennett & Plum, 1972). These patients are awake but not aware, although to unskilled observers they may be regarded as responsive and even sentient. This is because their eyes are open and can follow moving objects, while reflex withdrawal and grasping occur in the upper limbs.

More commonplace is the patient who is confused but can speak and hold brief exchanges that are meaningful to those around him – as when a patient is emerging from coma due to recent head injury or is going into coma from progressive brain disease. Discussions about competence for consent sometimes include references to intervals of lucidity during which consent might be secured. Such islands of clarity are far from the continuity of consciousness that puts the present moment in the context of memories of past experience and of contemplation of the future. Yet another common state is post-traumatic amnesia, when after head injury a person can seem to be fully alert and yet is not laying down any memory of current experience (Jennett & Teasdale, 1988).[1] This state usually lasts for only a few hours or days, but occasionally it continues for months. Such a patient will deny any memory of seemingly rational conversations carried on during this state, including statements to the police.

Consent for non-psychiatric therapy

Consent may be required for a variety of therapeutic interventions. For surgery, consent is traditionally sought no matter how trivial a procedure is planned. Yet consent is not usually obtained for various measures that can have much more serious implications – such as resuscitation, renal dialysis, or the initiation or continuation of other life-support measures under the general rubric of intensive care. Research is another matter – often less easily distinguished from therapy than might be realised.

These various medical procedures are frequently used without consent when an emergency arises and the patient is unable to refuse. They are also often embarked on as part of a stepwise process of treatment, for which consent is implied in the therapeutic relationship between doctor and patient. The assumption is that if the doctor decides that what is next needed is dialysis, or a certain drug, or a period on a ventilator, then the patient is not expected to argue – being very sick, even if fully conscious. I note in the Commissioner's documents that consent may be implied if the patient shows no sign of wishing to refuse treatment. However, as concern increases that the autonomy of patients be respected, there is increasing pressure to make more explicit to patients the benefits and burdens of alternative methods of management – including surgery. This question of patient choice was a central feature of the recent King's Fund consensus conference on the treatment of primary breast cancer (Consensus Development Conference, 1986).

Withholding and withdrawing 'heroic' interventions

Concern about 'heroic' measures being instituted or too-long continued is growing among the public – especially among those who are growing old

1. Reference added *post* symposium.

and those with chronic progressive diseases (Jennett, 1987).[1] They realise that when the time comes for rescue procedures, they may not be competent to refuse. This has led to the living will and right-to-die legislation in the USA. A recent review there showed that in practice such declarations were seldom invoked in legal terms when the time came (Eisendrath & Jonsen, 1983). Rather, the doctors and relatives were found to have taken the existence of such a document as giving them permission to consider management options within the framework of the patient's previously expressed wish to avoid 'heroic' measures unless there was a reasonable probability of survival for a reasonable time with a reasonable quality of life. Consider two papers in major American medical journals. Under the title ''Mercy – for the terminally ill cancer patient!'', a doctor recorded the enormous difficulty that he had had in restraining his colleagues from persisting with undignified and distressing treatment for his daughter (Beall, 1983). The other reported on 155 patients on long-term dialysis who had requested discontinuation of treatment so as to be allowed to die (Neu & Kjellstrand, 1986).

Also attracting increasing interest is consent for resuscitation and the status of 'Do not resuscitate' orders (Stephens, 1986). These have been commonplace in America for more than a decade but not one of the 300 intensive-care units in Britain appears yet to have a written code or set of guide-lines. That is not to say that such decisions are not made, but they are based on informal *ad hoc* agreements between doctors and nurses for each case as it arises (Baskett, 1986). Questioning patients surviving after successful resuscitation in one German intensive-care unit revealed that several of those who were >60 years of age wished they had not had their lives saved, even though they had been restored to a reasonable quality of life (Fusgen & Summa). Questioning patients, when admitted to hospital, about whether they would wish cardiopulmonary resuscitation to be instituted in the event of a crisis likewise revealed a substantial proportion who specifically recorded their wish not to be so rescued (Bedell & Delbanco, 1984). Yet when a crisis came, the doctors often overrode the previously expressed wishes of patients – believing that they had not really meant to refuse. A subsequent report concluded that suggestions that doctors should discuss resuscitation with patients who may die are unrealistic (Charlson *et al*, 1986).

I realise that these various examples of requests that specific treatment be withheld or withdrawn have perhaps more to do with the euthanasia debate than with that before us today. Nevertheless they do exemplify the complexity of consent for therapy – even when it promises to save or to prolong life. They also touch on whether consent comes in different forms. I would plead to retain the term 'informed consent' because it has become common usage. I cannot discern what advantage accrues from calling consent 'real' except that, as described by the Commission, this appears to be a lesser degree of consent.

---

1. Reference added *post* symposium.

Consent for research

Research covers a wide range of activities. These include epidemiology, definition of natural history, biological parameters, and studies on the effectiveness of therapy. The latter is now often designated 'Technology Assessment' and it has several stages of comprehensiveness including clinical trials and economic appraisal (Jennett, 1986). Perhaps it is the collection of data about biological parameters that causes most controversy about consent – because this may involve procedures that might not be done except for research purposes. Examples are cardiovascular monitoring, sampling body fluids, and imaging. This in turn raises the distinction between therapeutic and non-therapeutic research.

This is crucial in the present debate. From some recommendations, it might seem that almost anything is permissible provided it is labelled therapy. There is therefore an incentive for researchers so to designate their studies. The Medical Research Council (MRC) takes a broad view of what research can be regarded as therapeutic. This includes: new procedures that can benefit a patient by treatment, prevention, increased understanding; methods of prevention; novel procedures at the frontiers of knowledge; and trials with a placebo arm. The Canadian MRC has dropped the distinction between therapeutic and non-therapeutic research as being artificial and this might seem more honest. In the USA the National Commission on Biomedical and Behavioural Research suggests two questions to make the distinction (Mental Health Act Commission, 1985). Is this monitoring or measurement required or not for the well-being of the patient; and, does this therapy hold any prospect of benefit for this patient or not? The distinction between immediate and later benefit seems not to have been made. Given the lifelong nature of psychiatric illness, it seems to me quite possible that mentally ill persons could live to reap the benefit of research in which they themselves had participated years before.

The Guidelines of the British Paediatric Association are of interest in this context (British Paediatric Association Working Party, 1980). These assert that research is important for the benefit of children but that it should never be done on children if it could be done on adults. Declaring that non-therapeutic research is not necessarily either unethical or illegal, these guide-lines point out that such research may be needed both to benefit other children with the same condition and to add to basic knowledge. They emphasise the importance of recognising a sliding scale between the degree of benefit expected and the amount of discomfort and risk that is justified.

This is also an important feature of American adult practice, which relies heavily on institutional review boards (IRBs: equivalent to ethical committees in the UK). Originally they were required to approve research only if some risk was declared by the investigator, but since 1971 an IRB has to review all proposals. One purpose is to decide about whether any risk is involved and then to assess its degree and to consider whether it is justifiable to carry out the proposed research.

Two recent reports from America refer to specific efforts to deal with the difficult problem of consent for research in incompetent adults. One was about consent by proxy for research on elderly patients in nursing homes (Warren *et al*, 1986). The topic was to discover the benefit of keeping a long-term catheter in position, and the study was to involve only blood- and urine-sampling and plain X-rays of the abdomen. About half of 168 proxies refused consent for research on their elderly relatives, but a third of those who believed that the patient himself would have refused consent did give their consent. Many proxies who did not give consent for this particular research on their relatives were in favour of research in general, and also of research being done in hospital and on elderly patients themselves. Two-thirds of those who refused consent said, however, that they would have acted similarly whatever the nature of the research. It was believed by the investigators that this may have been because a nursing home, as distinct from a hospital, was considered an inappropriate place for research. Other reasons given were that the research would disturb the patient, that the patient himself would be likely to refuse, or that the proxy would not allow it to be done on himself.

These authors suggested that a greater degree of competence was needed for consent than for refusal, and that the higher the risk, the more stringent should the criteria be for competence. This seems to me almost as elusive a concept as the difference between informed and real consent proposed by the Commission. Another suggestion was the appointment of a 'consent auditor' to override proxy refusal when this seemed unjustified or against the patient's interest. It might be wondered how participation in research could be in the interests of elderly patients. The reason is a simple one, well known to those who have engaged in such research. When a group of such patients is recruited and studied in order to judge the effectiveness of some therapy, but only half of them are given this, there is often an unexpected improvement in the untreated group. In the absence of any placebo drug or procedure this is usually ascribed to the benefit to these patients of having more attention in general paid to them while they are the subjects of a study. A final suggestion was that patients with progressive dementing illnesses might be asked, while they are still competent, to consent in advance to participation in research at a later stage – rather like providing a living will.

The other report was about deferred consent for research on patients in coma being treated under emergency conditions after cardiac arrest (Abramson *et al*, 1986). A similar situation arises after severe head injury. It pointed out that exceptions to informed consent were now allowed under specific conditions. These are that the research would otherwise be impractical, that it involved minimal risk, that information was given once this was possible, and that the rights and welfare of the patient were protected. It considered that these applied to the dilemma of testing new treatments for serious brain damage. The authors emphasised that differential risk was an important principle – the additional risk associated with the research as compared with that of the condition itself when managed normally without a research component. Patients in this particular study had a very low likelihood of survival. Experimental treatment, or randomisation into a trial, was carried out without consent, but once relatives could be found, they were asked whether they were willing for participation to continue. An interesting comment on cultural differences was that it was much easier to gain cooperation for this multicentre study from units in European countries than in the USA – where one unit approached eventually refused to cooperate.

There can be no doubt about the need for research into mental illness and brain damage. If this is to be relevant to the relief of suffering and the reduction of avoidable death and disability, then research must at some stage involve patients with these conditions. It is, however, important to have a number of rules for clinical research – whether on volunteers or patients, competent or not, whether it is designated as therapeutic or not. I suggest six such rules for research: answer needed to good question; alternative means not possible; appropriate methods; acceptable risk; adequate numbers; and analysis valid statistically.

Only recently in America have four major mental-illness organisations of families and former patients joined together to sponsor initiatives that call for more scientific research. If this is to be helped rather than hindered, there will be need to reconsider the recommendation in the discussion document on consent. Dr Langley's (1986) response to Professor Kendell's (1986) misgivings seems to be that almost all research could be classified as therapeutic and would therefore be exempt from what Kendell had claimed to be the 'paralysing procedures' that have been proposed by the Commission. Yet Dr Langley seems to be subscribing to the sliding scale of risk and benefit to which I have referred – for he mentions interventions that are 'risky, or so invasive or dangerous as to be proscribed by the duty of care'. Certainly there seems a need to clarify whether a detailed rule book about research and consent is being written, or alternatively whether there is an intention to remind doctors of broad principles and to give them general guide-lines while putting faith in the guidance of local ethical committees. These are now available everywhere, but I note the reservation that they do not all behave consistently. But then neither do doctors, nor lawyers, nor anyone else among those who are nonetheless considered to be mentally competent.

References

ABRAMSON, N. S., MEISEL, A., & SAFAR, P. (1986) Deferred consent. *Journal of the American Medical Association (Chicago)*, **255**, 2466–2471.

BASKETT, P. J. F. (1986) The ethics of resuscitation. *Journal of the American Medical Association (Chicago)*, British Medical Journal, **293**, 189–190.

BEALL, J. A. (1983) Mercy – for the terminally ill cancer patient! *Journal of the American Medical Association*, **249**, 2883.

BEDELL, S. C. & DELBANCO, T. L. (1984) Choices about cardiopulmonary resuscitation in the hospital. *New England Journal of Medicine*, **310**, 1089–1093.

CHARLSON, M. E., SAX, E. L., MACKENZIE, R., FIELDS, S. D., BRAHAM, R. L. & DOUGLAS, JNR, R. G. (1986) Resuscitation: how do we decide? *Journal of the American Medical Association (Chicago)*, **255**, 1316–1322.

CONSENSUS DEVELOPMENT CONFERENCE (1986) Treatment of primary breast cancer. *British Medical Journal*, **293**, 946–947.

EISENDRATH, S. J. & JONSEN, A. R. (1983) The living will: help or hindrance? *Journal of the American Medical Association (Chicago)*, **249**, 2054–2058.

FUSGEN, I. & SUMMA, J.-D. (1978) How much sense is there in an attempt to resuscitate an aged person? *Gerontology*, **24**, 37–45.

JENNETT, B. (1986) *High Technology Medicine – Benefits and Burdens* (2nd edn). Oxford and New York: Oxford University Press.

——— (1987) Decisions to limit treatment. *The Lancet*, ii, 787–789.

——— & PLUM, F. (1972) Persistent vegetative state after brain damage. *The Lancet i*, 734–737.

——— & TEASDALE, G. M. (1988) *Management of Head Injuries* (2nd edn). Philadelphia: F. A. Davis.

KENDELL, R. E. (1986) The Mental Health Act Commission's 'Guidelines': a further threat to psychiatric research. *British Medical Journal*, **292**, 1249–1250.

LANGLEY, G. E. (1986) A threat to psychiatric research? *British Medical Journal*, **293**, 133–134.

MENTAL HEALTH ACT COMMISSION (1985) *Discussion Paper on Consent to Treatment*. London: Mental Health Act Commission.

NEU, S. & KJELLSTRAND, C. M. (1986) Stopping long-term dialysis: an empirical study of withdrawal of life-supporting treatment. *New England Journal of Medicine*, **314**, 14–20.

STEPHENS, R. L. (1986) Do not resuscitate orders: ensuring the patient's participation. *Journal of the American Medical Association (Chicago)*, **255**, 240–241.

THE BRITISH PAEDIATRIC ASSOCIATION WORKING PARTY (1980) Guidelines to aid ethical committees considering research involving children. *Archives of Disease in Childhood (London)*, **55**, 75–77.

WARREN, J. W., SOBAL, J., TENNEY, J. H., HOOPES, J. M., DAMRON, D., LEVENSON, S., DE FORGE, B. R. & MUNCIE, JNR, H. L. (1986) Informed consent by proxy: an issue in research with elderly patients. *New England Journal of Medicine*, **315**, 1124–1128.

5 Discussion

DR LANGLEY: I am grateful to Professor Jennett for pointing out that therapeutic research can have a broad definition. Certainly, that was very much in our minds, having read the Declaration of Helsinki and the MRC (Medical Research Council) publications. With these in mind, our suggestions or guide-lines may seem less inhibiting than when first read. Risk clearly is a subject that we did not deal with at any depth, but I think it is up to the ethics committees and other before-mentioned interested parties to establish this. Certainly our view on research was to take therapeutic research as broadly defined and that the use of that term would be not too inhibiting.

DR BIRLEY: I was very interested to hear the view that classifying research as therapeutic or non-therapeutic is a false distinction. I would subscribe to that and hope that we accept it. I think that all my research has been non-therapeutic and also that it has been non-invasive physically. On the other hand, it has involved very intimate invasive interviews of people and their families, which I would regard as just as threatening, and which is not covered at all by the law. Although I hope it will not be necessary, it may be best to have an ethical committee considering the uncertain nature of the law in this area. Also – and this point has been made by many people including Professor Michael Baum recently – nothing is more unethical than bad research. Thus, to do a badly designed therapeutic trial on patients, knowing that it will not produce the results from the design, is unethical. Therefore I would again put the case for having local ethical committees representing ethical and scientific concern, as better than having a higher authority.

MR SULLIVAN: May I respond to the last point that Professor Jennett made when he referred to the Commission's remark that local ethics committees appeared not to be acting consistently. I would read to you in answer a portion of the very latest report of the Institute of Medical Ethics (IME Bulletin, September 1986, suppl. 2):

> 'The results of the Institute's survey suggest that there is too much variation in the structure and working methods of research ethics committees in England and Wales for one to have any confidence that they are all doing an efficient and effective job.'

The report then bears witness to the good work that some research committees are doing, and goes on to say:

63

"The evidence of the survey shows, however, that some committees do not know to whom they are accountable, are circumvented by some researchers, either have no lay members or lay members who are not independent of the Health Service, have working practices that prevent them from fulfilling their functions and may not understand the legal requirements for informed consent."

I hope that is an, at least *ex post facto*, justification of what we said.

DR BEWLEY: We should consider the question of non-therapeutic invasive research, because that is obviously more difficult and there will be times when it might be highly desirable. If, for example, I go down with cerebral AIDS in 20 years' time it might be reasonable for somebody to do a brain biopsy. If I were asked today if I would have any objection to that, I would say 'no' in advance – provided it was a good piece of research, it was reasonable to do it, it was likely to show some results, and it had been accepted by a decent ethical committee. I am sure we can all agree today that one of the things that we are in favour of is ensuring that ethical committees that take these decisions are properly constituted and operate correctly. However, we should consider the hardest cases, or otherwise we will never establish the answer to some questions, for example, those involved in Alzheimer's disease.

PROFESSOR JENNETT: I think the last point raised by Dr Bewley is interesting because the American report on the nursing-home demented patients (Warren *et al*, 1986, *see* p. 62) raised the issue of whether people with a chronic dementing illness might not be asked for consent for research in the future, rather as in the cases of the 'living will' and the 'right to die'; exactly as Dr Bewley suggests. The question of the ethical committees is an important one, and the GMC (General Medical Council) and BMA (British Medical Association) are looking at this. Should there be some central ethical committee for referral of hard cases and for setting standards and ensuring that there is adequate ethical scrutiny?

6 Psychiatric implications

ELAINE MURPHY

Psychiatrists have always had to face major dilemmas in managing the day-to-day care of incapable patients. As doctors, we are concerned to ensure that patients receive the treatment they need. An important limitation in achieving that aim is that a patient's mental disorder may so cloud his or her judgement that he is unable to appreciate what is in his own best interests. Under those circumstances, doctors generally believe that they have not only the right, but a duty, to ensure that the patient receives proper treatment for his or her restoration to a state of mind in which he can reliably decide what is best for himself. If restoration to mental health is impossible, then the doctor has a duty to ensure that the patient achieves his maximum potential for leading a satisfactory life adapted to his residual handicaps with the least possible physical and mental distress, by means of proper rehabilitation and care.

Psychiatrists who work solely with elderly people are treating patients of whom approximately two-thirds will be unable to give real consent to treatment. One of the main features of dementia is that reasoning and judgement are impaired at an early stage. However all psychiatrists are familiar with the day-to-day practical problems of consent to treatment in patients with a major psychosis in which suspiciousness, fear, or delusional beliefs impair judgement and influence rational decision-making.

The draft code of practice and *Consent to Treatment* documents published by the Mental Health Act Commission tackled the dilemmas involved by an essentially legalistic approach, suggesting that good practice lay in balancing two opposing basic rules of common law. The first basic rule is that any form of physical treatment or care applied without the patient's consent is a trespass or 'battery', a wrong against the physical person; a patient can bring an action alleging battery if real consent has not been obtained. The second basic rule is that anyone proposing to give treatment to a patient is under a duty to use reasonable care and skill. A doctor performs his duty of care if he acts in accordance with a practice rightly accepted as proper by a responsible body of skilled and experienced doctors. To fail to

65

give proper treatment and care is negligence and a patient can bring an action alleging negligence if he can prove he has suffered damage resulting from the doctor's failure to give adequate care. Common law is supplemented by specific statute law about the circumstances when consent to treatment as defined in the Mental Health Act 1983 may be dispensed with.

The major difficulty for psychiatrists in this legalistic approach is that it appears to give no guidance on the day-to-day practical problems which we face in real life when treating incapable patients. I would like to look at one or two case examples of very common situations which will be familiar to most psychiatrists:

> Mrs Smith has always been an isolated, independent and rather testy character who was admitted to hospital for treatment of pneumonia after having been found in a collapsed state by her home help. Her insidious dementia has been coming on for the past 2 years and it is becoming increasingly obvious that she is not coping at home alone. Mrs Smith is sometimes incontinent; there is the odd accident when she fails to find the ward WC. Mrs Smith does not, however, like bathing or changing. When she came into hospital it appeared she had not changed her clothes for several months. There is no doubt that for the sake of the rest of the ward patients and staff, Mrs Smith has to be persuaded firmly, and sometimes with the nurses physically carrying her to the bathroom, to be cleaned and changed.

Now according to the *Consent to Treatment* document, every time one of the nurses gives personal care to Mrs Smith, who is on occasions vociferously reluctant, the nurse is committing the offence of battery.

> Mrs Brown also has dementia. She believes the ward is the biscuit factory she worked in all her life; she spends her day collecting up objects from all over the ward and placing them in a box; she appears to be packing biscuits. At five o'clock every evening she wants to 'go home', to 'cook her husband's tea'. Her husband died many years ago. She repeatedly makes for the door and would be out in the street in a flash if we let her. Every evening a nurse spends a long time persuading, cajoling, diverting her attention, and sometimes physically steering her away from the door.

Is this committing another battery? I could repeat a hundred instances like this where day-to-day treatment and care are given to reluctant patients, against their will, but with the intention to fulfil the duty of care to incapable patients.

There is a missing dimension from this legal approach. First it ignores the spirit of intention of the action, and second, the manner in which it is carried out. The nature of the interchange between a patient and a professional carer has long been governed by professional standards and informal codes of practice, which are maintained by professional training and good example. It is not enough that we balance in our minds opposing pieces of common law; we must make explicit the importance of the style of behaviour and emotional tone in our dealings with patients. Good practice will not be established by balancing legal niceties, but by consensus within the professions and the general public about what ought to be expected of professional carers in relation to incapable patients.

Safeguards for treating incapable patients

The Commission points out in its *Consent to Treatment* document that the treatment of incapable patients has not been expressly dealt with by the law and the Commission is attempting to predict what line the courts would take. They suggest that, if possible, an incapable patient should not have to be detained under the Mental Health Act if protection comparable to statutory protection can be provided. A series of safeguards are suggested. Safeguard one is that the doctor should discuss the proposed treatment with one or more relatives. No-one would disagree with this; it is accepted good practice now. However, the Commission has a rather rosy view of relatives. While the majority of caring relatives only want what is in the best interests of the patient and make a valuable contribution to discussions on treatment, a substantial minority of relatives put their own best interests before those of the patient. It is not uncommon for the children of elderly patients to have more of an eye on the early prospects of inheriting property than on what is most likely to benefit the elderly person. More frequent, though, is the problem of the caring family who have multiple opinions of what ought to be done. There may be three or four children who have been at loggerheads all their lives, waging their own private war over the sick elderly person.

The problem of disagreeing relatives is highlighted further in the problems of treating children and adolescents. A very high proportion of minors requiring treatment have separated or divorced parents. We all know that children are often the focus for parental disputes. How far should the treating psychiatrist consult and hear both parents in these cases? The discussion documents are not helpful on this issue at all. The *Consent to Treatment* document suggests that a minor over the age of 16 but under the age of 18 can be treated against his wishes with the parents' consent – if his fears of treatment are due to 'youthful fears' or 'lack of experience'. This needs some clarifying and may not be a legally sound way of dispensing with an older minor's consent. The issue of parental authority and at what age it ceases to take primacy over an adolescent's wishes is one of course we have all followed with interest in the case of the prescription of contraceptive pills for girls under 16 years old. The same kinds of problems arise in 15-year-olds who have taken overdoses or have other problems relating to their development as adults; sometimes it will clearly not be in the child's best interests to inform the parents.

Returning to the 'safeguards' for treating incapable patients, the second safeguard is that the doctor should give due weight to the observations and opinions of members of other disciplines involved in treatment 'but the ultimate responsibility will nevertheless remain his'. Most psychiatrists will have no difficulty with this. The multiprofessional case conference is the usual forum for decision-making. The third safeguard is that the doctor should invite a written second opinion from a consultant or an established GP. This may be helpful in making a decision on a specific physical treatment, but is hardly practical for day-to-day care. Safeguard four is for use when an incapable patient refuses treatment. In this case, the Commission would like an appointed second opinion to consult in the manner prescribed for detained patients, a cumbersome and expensive business, which I would suggest is highly unlikely to happen except in very particular circumstances. The fifth safeguard merely indicates that where surgical treatment is being considered, the surgeon and another doctor (GP or psychiatrist) should consult with each other about it. Again, this is usual practice and not controversial.

The main point to take issue with is that these 'safeguards' or rules are imposed on a profession that has not evolved and agreed them from within its own ranks. It is always difficult to predict how common law will be interpreted, but it is possible that a 'responsible body of skilled and experienced doctors' might not agree that slavish attention to the Commission's safeguards was necessary for the proper discharge of one's duty of care. Rules of good practice must evolve from within the profession, in consultation with others, and should not be imposed by some external body.

Research with patients suffering mental disorder

In spite of major advances in pharmacological and other treatment for serious psychiatric disorders in the past half century, a general psychiatrist's work is largely with patients whose lives are blighted for many years with chronic, disabling, and distressing conditions for which there is at present no cure. Some disorders, such as the dementias, are fatal. The human and economic burden of psychiatric disorders will remain until we have an understanding of the contributions of biological and psychosocial factors to the onset and course of these illnesses and are able to develop rational treatments. It is only through research that headway is going to be made. Improvements in quality of care by the use of better nursing skills, by refining techniques of rehabilitation, and by investing money into providing a better physical and emotional environment for the patients, are undoubtedly the key areas in which resources need to be directed for today's patients, but any real reduction in suffering will only be achieved by prevention or cure as a result of research.

There are many obstacles to the pursuit of research into psychiatric disorders. Probably the most important is the low priority accorded to this field by public and private grant-giving agencies, and also, sadly, by a lack of commitment by busy clinicians already overburdened by the clinical service demands on their time. The geographical separation of research departments that have the skills to pursue promising avenues (largely the teaching hospitals and postgraduate institutes) from the places where the patients are (mental hospitals, district general hospitals, and 'out there in the community') makes collaborative research ventures extremely difficult to establish successfully. In other words, the catchment-area psychiatrist has enough on his plate without troubling too much about finding 'research subjects' for the academic department 10 miles away. A further and potentially very damaging threat to research was contained within the documents published by the Mental Health Act Commission.

The ethics of research with patients incapable of giving consent has been considered in some detail in the past by the Medical Research Council (1963) and Royal College of Physicians (1984) and forms the stuff of discussions at independent health-authority and medical-school ethics committees on all occasions when research protocols involve patients with mental illness and mental handicap. As a society, we readily acknowledge the risk that overenthusiastic researchers will sacrifice the comfort and dignity of current patients for the possibility of benefit for future generations of sufferers. As a consequence, the medical and scientific professions in this country have created within their own professional organisations a consensus view of what is acceptable and what is not. Values and opinions differ between one ethical committee and another, as anyone who has had the experience of submitting the same protocol to several different district ethical committees will know. In general, however, a consensus view of what is proper will be arrived at without too much difficulty. At the present time, there is no evidence that unwarranted investigations or procedures are being conducted on patients with mental handicap or mental illness, nor is there any evidence that dedicated researchers are exploiting patients for the sole benefit of research.

Many psychiatrists were surprised, then, to see research activities mentioned by the consultation documents *Consent to Treatment* and the draft code of practice. There was surprise that the Commission regarded the field of research as coming within its terms of reference. The membership of the Commission has clearly not been constructed with that area in mind. Although some members of the Commission have engaged in research, most of the psychiatrists on it are clinicians whose professional lives have been spent largely in clinical service, an appropriate background for the Commission's role with detained patients, but without expertise in the area of research. The ethical and moral dilemmas of conducting research are well understood by the Commission and indeed the *Code of Practice* para. 4.13.6 provides a balanced and comprehensive list of the variables which need to be taken into account and weighed by those undertaking clinical research programmes. Paragraph 4.13.6 is quoted here:

> "Whoever proposes a clinical research programme involving a mental health patient, and the Ethical Committee which considers it, must weigh up and balance the many variables, including:
> whether or not the patient is capable of giving a real consent;
> the likelihood of benefit to the patient;
> whether the research will actually advance knowledge and experience;
> whether that knowledge could be obtained by other means;
> the extent of the experimental intervention;
> the amount of distress which will or may be caused;
> whether the risks have already been identified and the safety of the patient sufficiently protected;
> whether the investigator is adequately experienced and qualified and has the necessary facilities."

The theoretical principles, then, have been expounded very clearly. It is on the practical side of implementing these sound principles that the consultation documents are at fault. The documents are phrased in such a way that they could be interpreted strictly as stopping all research with patients who could not give consent. Even if the guide-lines are interpreted in the most liberal way possible, the series of 'safeguards' are likely to prevent researchers proceeding up the 'yellow brick road of research' and are so restrictive and expensive, that the most energetic and determined researcher will simply lose heart and give up.

The first problem arises in relation to the Commission's concept of a typology of research. Three main kinds of research are distinguished: (a), physical interventions e.g. ECT, drugs by injection, surgery; (b) pharmacological intervention e.g. drugs given orally; and (c) psychosocial interventions e.g. psychotherapy, behaviour therapy. Sometimes, however, research investigations are carried out as part of the normal routine clinical investigations that the patient would receive as an aid to his personal treatment. This is referred to as 'incidental' research. For example, using blood samples taken in the course of routine tests following admission to hospital for the purpose of a research investigation may be called 'incidental', presumably unless the quantity of blood taken is beyond what would normally be taken for routine tests.

A further type of research is referred to by the commission as 'purely descriptive'. This is not clearly defined, but two examples are given, 'a study of case records' and 'epidemiology', which the commission feels are beyond its remit. This may be comforting to the epidemiologists, but it is not clear, for example, what would be the status of research that involved long mental-status interviews, psychometric tests, audiometric recordings,

EEG recordings, or brain scans using new painless, probably harmless, but rather tedious procedures which may, if insensitively carried out, be rather more irksome for the subject than a simple blood test.

A further distinction is made between 'therapeutic' research, where it may or may not benefit the patient who takes part in it, and 'non-therapeutic' research, which is not intended to benefit the individual. It is 'non-therapeutic' research that 'warrants the greatest care and safeguards'. Most research into psychiatric disorders seems to fall into the latter category. However, the distinction between 'therapeutic' and 'non-therapeutic' research is misleading. Any research that leads to a better understanding of the patient's condition is part of the doctor's obligation to his patient and hence part of the therapeutic role. A more appropriate and acceptable distinction would be that between research that is directly relevant to the type of condition the patient is suffering from and research that is not relevant but in which the patient participates, usually as a volunteer. Perhaps a more simple but acceptable rule should be that patients who are unable to consent should not participate in research that is not relevant to their illness. Furthermore there should be explicit emphasis on eliminating research which carries a potential for discomfort, hazard, or harm beyond what would normally be involved in the routine clinical treatment of the patient's condition.

The Commission, however, has suggested that all non-therapeutic research is unacceptable in patients who are incapable, even where the patient 'consents', thus at a stroke outlawing most research with patients with severe psychosis, the dementias, or mental handicap, and with children and minors.

Research into, and increased understanding of, a condition often leads unexpectedly to benefits for individual patients and points the way to some important advance in treatment. The research identification of a biological marker to identify carriers of Huntington's chorea would never have happened if it had not been possible to study the patients themselves as a first preliminary step. The study of metabolites of cerebral amines in blood, urine, and CSF [cerebrospinal fluid] in patients with manic–depressive illness has helped focus the pharmaceutical companies' research efforts on finding more selective antidepressant medication that reduces unwanted side-effects. There are dozens of examples where research would never have happened if the Commission's rules had applied.

The Mental Health Act Commission was established to monitor and oversee the implementation of the act and has a special role in relation to protecting the rights of detained patients in hospital. However, the Commission clearly has ambitions to expand its brief. Their guide-lines on research 'apply as much to general practice as to hospital practice. They should be used as much for informal patients as detained patients'. It follows that the guide-lines would apply to research into all forms of psychiatric disorder, however minor. While agreeing with the Commission that special care is required in acquiring real consent to treatment and in research with patients with any form of mental disorder, I think that the notion that all non-therapeutic research is unacceptable in mildly emotionally disturbed patients in general practice who are fully capable of giving real consent without implementing a long list of tedious safeguards is overprotective and stigmatising, and merely serves to perpetuate the myth that mental patients are different and have less right to make decisions for themselves than other patients. It is hard to believe that this is what the Commission intended.

Let us turn now to the 'safeguards' which the Commission proposes should apply to all research with mentally disordered patients. The first two safeguards will cause no difficulty as they are already accepted practice. These are: that all research should be considered by a properly constituted local ethics committee; and that the ethics committee and researcher should ruminate over the pros and cons listed above from paragraph 4.13.6 of the code of practice. The third safeguard is that there should be 'a higher standard of certainty' of the patient's consent to take part in a research project than when 'ordinary treatment is in question'. The philosophical and ethical reasons for accepting by implication a lower standard of what is 'real' consent for treatment than research are not clear and seem ethically unacceptable. The fourth safeguard is the one that in practice would prevent most research projects getting off the ground: 'Where non-therapeutic research is proposed, a second opinion should be obtained from a consultant as to the capacity of the patient to consent and the reality of his consent'. Imagine what this would mean in practice. Kendell (1986) gave an excellent example of how this rule would affect research in practice. No longer would a consultant who wished to take blood samples from a hundred or so out-patients simply get ethical approval and then ask his patient's permission. A second consultant would have to interview every patient to establish whether the patient was capable of giving 'real consent'. This would be impossibly tedious and expensive. Much valuable research into mental disorder has been done by scientists in other disciplines – neurologists, biochemists, sociologists. Are these researchers going to be subjected to the same rules to curtail their activities? Consultant psychiatrists would be in great demand giving second opinions on 'capability to consent'! Pity the poor old epidemiologist who wants to take blood samples from several hundred community-dwelling subjects with depression. The budget necessary to pay travelling expenses and fees for 'second opinions' would soon drain the coffers of most research funds. The fifth safeguard is equally contentious; that the relatives of the patient should be fully informed, with the patient's consent (whenever he can give it). 'Their concurrence in the patient's participation should be obtained if possible'.

It is clearly important that where a patient is incapable of consent, relatives should be consulted closely at every stage of treatment and whenever research is being considered. But when a patient is perfectly capable of making his own decision, it is both unnecessary and stigmatising to ask to confirm the decision with a relative. Once again, patients with psychiatric disorder are singled out for paternalistic control, quite contrary to the spirit of the 1983 Act.

Conclusion

The issue of consent to treatment concerns all clinicians working in the medical and allied professions. In the field of psychiatric disorder, this area is of special concern also to social workers and to relatives. It is the family that largely bears the brunt of the distress caused by continuing untreated psychiatric disorder. Most psychiatrists welcome the debate on consent to treatment and many would like guide-lines on tackling the problem of treating and caring for incapable patients and in the conduct of research. But the Mental Health Act Commission is not equipped to do this job on its own. It is not sufficient that many members of the Commission are psychiatrists. The Commission needs to establish credibility with the psychiatric profession and other interested parties such as the nursing profession, social workers, and those voluntary organisations campaigning for better treatment and care such as the National Schizophrenia Fellowship, MIND, and the Alzheimer's Disease Society. Any guide-lines should have the unequivocal support of the Royal Colleges, the British Association of Social Workers, and voluntary bodies. The only way to achieve that is for these organisations to be directly involved in the working parties that draft the documents. It is in the patients' best interests that common ground is established between the caring professions, the Mental Health Act Commission and the general public.

References

KENDELL, R. E. (1986) The Mental Health Act Commission's "Guidelines"; a further threat to psychiatric research. *British Medical Journal*, **292**, 1249–1250.
MEDICAL RESEARCH COUNCIL (1963) Responsibility in investigations on human subjects. *The Medical Research Council* 1962–3. London: HMSO (Cmnd. 2382).
ROYAL COLLEGE OF PHYSICIANS OF LONDON (1984) *Guidelines on the Practice of Ethics Committees in Medical Research*. London: Royal College of Physicians.

Acknowledgements

The preparation of this paper was particularly influenced by previous work by Professor R. E. Kendell, Dr J. R. Hamilton, Professor S. R. Hirsch, and Dr R. G. Jezzard.

6 Discussion

PROFESSOR HIRSCH: I should like to introduce a fresh notion, which is relevant to Professor Murphy's paper. The differentiation of research into therapeutic and non-therapeutic perhaps arose partially from the original MRC (1962) guide-lines. They made this distinction but included under 'therapeutic' anything that would contribute to an understanding of the patient's condition. The topic was not elaborated, however, and the document then went on to deal with research with volunteers, who would be typical 'people in the street', who did not suffer from any relevant condition, undergoing various tests.

I suggest, therefore, that confusion arises when research on volunteers, to whom the research is not directly relevant, is considered as non-therapeutic research. I think the main distinction should be that therapeutic research is relevant to the patient and the class of patients that is suffering from his or her condition, and that non-therapeutic research is performed on volunteers, and is not relevant to the volunteers' condition in any way. Others argue that any research that bears on the understanding of a patient's condition is potentially therapeutic because the knowledge gained may lead to thera-peutic advantage. The advances made in treatment and prevention of problems associated with the Rh factor developed within 10 years of original research on butterflies, and were not foreseen by the research workers. There are other examples.

I wonder if this kind of distinction could be accepted? Would others contribute to a consensus of opinion that any research that is relevant to the patient's condition is therapeutic?

DR LANGLEY: There is not a great deal of difference between the point of view that Professor Hirsch has just expressed and the Commission's view, if one takes a fairly liberal definition of what is therapeutic, although I would point out that Professor Hirsch's is not really the Commission's view of what is therapeutic and non-therapeutic, as we adopted the already-quoted definition from the Declaration of Helsinki.

In answer to earlier suggestions as to whether the Commission acted outside its remit, I can only say that we were responding to a great number of inquiries we were receiving. Whether or not we were right to do so, we were merely trying to be helpful.

Concerning Professor Murphy's examples, I am, as a fellow psychogeriatrician, concerned about the issues of battery, but I feel one has to take the balancing duty of care. That is relatively easy when treatment alone is concerned, but more difficult when one is doing research, where the duty of care may operate in the opposite direction.

MRS TERESA S. MYERS: I think there is a sad tendency in human nature only to question competence when somebody is disagreeing with you. The idea of deferred consent is excellent because it allows the doctor to achieve something that he or she might otherwise not be able to at a more advanced state of disease. However, in the USA at least, we have found that all kinds of deferred consents or advanced directives such as living wills, Natural Death Act directives, durable powers of attorney for health care, and a number of other methods that we have devised to extend the patient's autonomy, are not followed, because the doctors do not agree with them. So I think you have to examine the whole basis of consent. If you are going to accept one thing from a patient you had best look at the rest of the range of possibilities that the patient might ask for. In our country, at least, we are finding a difficulty with the medical profession accepting some and not the others.

MR SULLIVAN: I welcome Professor Murphy's talk. She has discussed core problems about practical situations and what can be done about them to assure not only doctors, but other people, as to what is being done to incapable patients. She cited certain examples such as a nurse steering a patient towards a necessary place! Particularly in the light of what the Court of Appeal has since said this year about what is acceptable in the ordinary conduct of human life, I should think that the law would have very little indeed to say. Such cases fall outside the limits of the principle that I dealt with earlier.

Another useful example is that of the patient who has a physical condition not related at all to a mental-state disorder. It may well have been an omission on our part in not dealing with it, perhaps because we saw the difficulties involved. I think Professor Murphy is suggesting that the document be improved in that respect so that some assistance is given to the doctors in avoiding problems by knowing in advance what the courts' views would be. The code that the Commission produced was put out in accordance with our statutory duty as a draft with the hope that all involved parties would amend it. It was a draft which we would have put out for consultation if we had not been bound by statute to put it out to the Secretary of State.

Finally, to take up Professor Hirsch's point, I think the debate as to whether the non-therapeutic/therapeutic distinction is the right one, or whether there is some other, is the sort that should be encouraged. I will not express any view about his suggestion; it may be right, it may be wrong as far as I am concerned. I would only say that the difference between 'therapeutic' and 'non-therapeutic' has a far longer history than just the Medical Research Council's documents in 1962 or 1964. It goes back to all the previous pronouncements which I mentioned, such as, for example, the Nuremberg Code, the Helsinki Declaration, and so on.

PROFESSOR MURPHY: One of my major problems is that while steering the old lady to the bathroom is one thing, taking kicking and screaming schizophrenic patients who have taken overdoses to the casualty department to have their stomachs washed out is another and we might be unhappy with the way we intervene. There is no doubt that the more we talk to members of the Commission about their interpretation of what they have written, the nearer it seems to come into line with what we need. However, I think we shall need guide-lines on the guide-lines, becauses the nurses are now anxious. Nurses and others in a team are saying, 'I've locked the door because Mrs Smith is trying to get out. Can I do that? And for how long should I do it? Can we just do it during the drug round or should we open it up again?'. We shall have to deal with all these issues if we are to get a usable working document.

7 Protection for the patient: the plight of patients and their families

DOROTHY SILBERSTON

There have been important changes in the climate of opinion about the issue of patient protection, which are reflected in the provisions of the 1983 Mental Health Act. The 1959 Act had no sections about consent to treatment. Safeguards for the patient were all to do with compulsory admission and detention. The responsible medical officer could and did treat patients as he thought best, and the use of new drugs together with the policy shift to care in the community led to thousands of discharges from our mental hospitals. Discussions about amendment of the 1959 Act took place when those claiming to speak for detained patients began to be concerned about civil liberty and the right to refuse treatment. At this time, the National Schizophrenia Fellowship was founded. It would probably never have come into being but for the consequences of the run-down of the mental hospitals, and the difficulty, sometimes the impossibility, of getting any treatment or care for a relative who seemed in desperate need of it. For there was a growing reluctance among psychiatrists throughout the 1970s to admit patients to hospital and to give treatment. Among nurses, there was anxiety about restraining patients who tried to walk out of hospital when they seemed desperately ill. This developed from many people's loathing of the old mental hospitals, and from heated objections to any form of institutional care – which continue to this day. Concomitantly, there were attacks on the psychiatrists based in these institutions. Partly this was a reflection of a changing view of doctors in general; there was a greater readiness to sue them if mistakes were made, and they were accused of authoritarianism and paternalism. In some quarters, there was concern about the overprescribing of drugs, worry about taking any drugs at all, and about possible side-effects, and far more interest in alternative medicine.

Psychiatry was affected by this general climate, and also by other popular opinions. In addition to the general denigration of the role of drugs, there was the view that mental illness has no basis in chemical malfunction in the brain, or other physical causes, but is due to family tensions or adverse social conditions, for which drugs provide no answer. There was also the historic caricature of psychiatrists as 'headshrinkers' and the occurrence of sane dissidents being treated as if they were mentally ill in the USSR. Thus suspicion began to fall on the work of all doctors in this field. The 'anti-psychiatry' movement has resulted in the formation of the Campaign against Psychiatric Oppression, and the British Network of Alternatives to Psychiatry, in the last two years. It is against this background that concerned members of the public see the issues of consent to treatment and protection for the incapable patient.

For the ordinary person, going to a general practitioner (GP), seeing a specialist, or entering hospital, means that he or she wants advice or practical help. To get that help, he or she expects to be examined, and then treated – why go otherwise? In the National Consumer Council's *Patients' Rights* leaflet, this is regarded as a reasonable working assumption for doctors, although the text goes on to advise readers that they can decide whether to accept the treatment proposed or not, and can stop having it at any time. The doctor would presumably try to reason with the patient if treatment seemed likely to help, but if persuasion failed, would infer that he or she was in their right mind, and however foolishly, could take his or her own decisions and be left to live or die with the consequences.

In psychiatric cases, problems about consent to treatment arise with a small minority of GPs who take the view that if a person who is physically capable of getting to the surgery will not attend, nothing can be done. What of the person that, to everyone around him or her, appears to have lost his or her senses? If such a person can no longer work, neglects himself and his children, wastes money, turns on friends, etc., who would not call on a doctor for help, despite the fact that the person concerned is against this? Family members feel desperate and abandoned if doctors, in these circumstances, are not willing to make a home visit. This is the first practical problem in the 'consent to treatment' conflict. A second problem arises if a GP does visit and fails to persuade the person to accept any treatment or see a psychiatrist, or judges that the situation is too serious for delay and arranges admission to hospital on a compulsory basis.

The informal psychiatric patient must in theory be treated like any other patient, free to leave hospital (as many do by discharging themselves), free to visit a GP or psychiatrist or not, and free to refuse treatment. This theory breaks down with the geriatric patient suffering, for example, from dementia, or the mentally handicapped person incapable of making judgements. To deal with all these areas would take too long, and I am not competent to do so. I shall therefore consider only the problem of the adult psychiatric patient who seems able to choose whether or not to seek informal admission, but who has become unable to cope with life. When such a person refuses medical help and is then admitted to hospital and detained there compulsorily, in the interests of his health or safety or to protect others, the question of compulsory treatment arises. Similar problems can arise when he refuses treatment when living outside hospital.

Members of the public see these problems as questions of practical alternatives. Compulsory admission to hospital is repugnant to most people. Nevertheless, on balance, it seems a better alternative than no action at all. Do we ignore illness, because the person concerned believes he is not ill, while watching his life collapsing around him? Is there any point in admitting such people to hospital unless treatment is given, compulsorily if need be? The alternative is to allow further deterioration. With drug treatment, we know that many patients can improve considerably, while others benefit dramatically from ECT. Although these treatments are not a cure, they do arrest and reverse the process of deterioration, in the majority of cases, at least for a time. If no action is taken, either to admit to hospital compulsorily or, once there, to proceed with compulsory treatment if necessary, what are the alternatives for those, usually members of the person's family, that are in the middle of the precipitating events? Often, these people – spouses, parents, siblings, may find it impossible to live with the affected person. Wives and husbands may bring divorce actions, but are there to be injunctions, etc., to preclude such people from their homes? I believe the availability of voluntary or compulsory admission to hospital when recurring relapses develop, as they do in so many cases of schizophrenia, will often determine whether or not the patient retains his place in the family home and long-term support from family members.

We should consider the Mental Health Act Commission's eagerness to see guardianship used far more, as an alternative to compulsory admission. If this is realistic, who would not welcome it? Guardianship implies provision of a place for a discharged psychotic patient to live – provision that, in many parts of the country, is scanty, not available at all, or unsuitable. It also means that social-services departments or individuals have to take on heavy duties. Since the 1959 Act introduced the concept of guardianship, very few legal orders have been made, I suggest that because the legal regulations governing guardianship impose so many conditions, few local authorities feel they can meet them, given staff limitations and cost, and few individuals want to undertake daunting legal responsibilities for someone who is often difficult, hostile, or unpredictable, and unwilling, or unable, to accept the imposed conditions of residence or occupation. Guardianship, therefore, does not seem a viable alternative to compulsory admission.

Letting affected people live outside hospital often could be such an alternative, but for one problem: that of relapse apparently resulting from failure to take drugs by mouth or injection. Before the McCullough judgement in 1985 this problem was often dealt with by a renewal of compulsory powers, but this is now ruled illegal (Regina *vs* Hallstrom and Another; Regina *vs* Gardiner and Another, 1985). Again, members of the public are faced with a dilemma. We, as professionals, know that all drugs have side-effects, and that sufferers from schizophrenia often violently object to them, and fear possible long-term consequences of taking them. We see that drugs usually help with more acute symptoms, and are terrified when out-patients decide to refuse injections or stop taking drugs orally, as we know what the result is likely to be. The consequences of relapse may include weeks or months in hospital, or deterioration resulting in loss of rented accommodation and subsequently in wandering, sleeping rough, theft, and eventually, a prison sentence. Against these consequences, we must consider the patient's wish to refuse treatment, and the unknown future effects of drugs used. To enable as many relapsing psychotic patients as possible to live outside hospital, and to forestall or deal quickly with deterioration, the National Schizophrenia Fellowship is urging the Secretary of State to introduce legislation, with safeguards, to enable doctors to prescribe drugs for out-patients on a compulsory basis.

There are many more safeguards for the incapable patients contained in the 1983 Act; there are more controls over compulsory admission, new provisions about consent to treatment etc, and more. Tribunals are convened. The ordinary member of the public does not know how these safeguards are working in practice, as they have only been operating for a few years. Now the McCullough judgement and the draft code of practice prepared by the Mental Health Act Commission introduce many more safeguards. Consideration of the balance between compulsory admission and treatment, and safeguards for the incapable patient, is a major concern of the code. Unfortunately, its incredibly complex language is very difficult for a lay person, perhaps for anyone, to understand, but I make the following observations:

1. how impractical many of the recommendations are, given the staff, facilities, and resources in and outside hospital available to implement them
2. how it ignores the highly disturbed mental state of the newly admitted patient, that he or she cannot absorb information, let alone understand it, or judge his or her best interests, until treatment clears his or her mind
3. how much weight it gives to the opinions of social workers and hospital managers, none of whom have any training in prescribing or treatment, or take any responsibility, ultimately, for the patient
4. how difficult, if not impossible it would be for doctors to observe the recommendations about consent to treatment, such is their complexity; anxiety about transgressing some detail could mean no action is taken
5. how far it tips the balance towards the patient's right to decide what treatment he wants, despite the fact that need for treatment was the primary reason for hospital admission
6. how little it takes account of the effect on others, e.g. in the home, when someone has a severe psychotic illness.

Is the Commission's vision of a patient, helpless at the hands of predatory relatives, who 'are not bound by law to have the patient's best interests at heart', of doctors keen to employ drugs as a means of social control, compatible with reality? There will always be callous relatives and incompetent professionals in every sphere, but all the evidence of the past 25 years shows that patients are not kept in psychiatric hospitals under medical control as they once were. And it is doctors who have taken the overwhelming majority of decisions to discharge patients.

Many members of the public now feel that, far from needing more protection from compulsory admission and treatment, the incapable patient needs protection from premature discharge with no plan for the next stage of living, and no after-care. In 1976, the Salvation Army's annual report drew attention to the large numbers of mentally disturbed people in its hostels, and to the stream of patients discharged without adequate preparation and 'expected to re-enter society and cope with the demands of daily living'. Many were totally incapable of doing so. 'The vast majority' the Army said 'became rootless wanderers, unemployable, frequently charged with criminal offences'. This remains the fate of many suffering from chronic psychotic illness. Our aim, surely, must be to enable doctors, families, and others to do their utmost to prevent this outcome: first, by acting on the Undersecretary of State at the Department of Health and Social Security's 1986 statement to Parliament: 'We expect clinicians to satisfy themselves (before a patient leaves hospital) that there are appropriate support facilities . . . outside the hospital'; second, by making admission less difficult at times of relapse. Here I must mention the inaccurate description of the Mental Health Act's conditions for compulsory admission, in one of the standard pyschiatric textbooks (Gelder *et al*, 1983), which may be contributing to these problems. Third, by receiving into hospital the violent, disruptive, and chronically ill patient who is not acceptable in any of the alternative forms of shelter, whether group homes, hostels, or the family home, as his or her only alternative otherwise will be to live rough, surviving or not surviving. Fourth, by doctors not shrinking from admission or treatment without consent if that seems the only way to prevent deterioration. In the long term, we want more effective drugs, with fewer side-effects. To find such cures, we must have research, but I understand the draft code would make research more difficult, if not impossible. The public could never support that, although agreeing that safeguards are needed and preferring research involving patients who can give consent.

We all see doctors as absolutely indispensable in research as in treatment. For every other illness it is doctors we turn to first, and so it is for psychiatric illness. Looking once more at practical alternatives, there is no other profession in which we could have confidence, although many give valuable help, as do non-professionals. We do not want to see doctors so restricted by regulations and safeguards that they will neither act decisively and quickly – often important in this field – nor wish to treat the most difficult patients.

References

GELDER, M., GATH, D. & MAYOU, R. (1983) *The Oxford Textbook of Psychiatry* (reprinted with corrections 1986). Oxford: Oxford University Press.

Cases cited

REGINA *vs* HALLSHOM and ANOTHER, ex parte W; REGINA *vs* GARDINER and ANOTHER, *ex parte* L. (20 December 1985).

7 Discussion

DR R. N. PALMER: I am on the secretariat of the Medical Protection Society and I suffer the double handicap of being qualified in both medicine and law. I would like to consider and reinforce points made by Professor Murphy and Mrs Silberston. I think we have seen some evidence that some health authorities are already beginning to treat the draft code as though it were the Secretary of State's 'gospel'. I think the draft code is unfortunate or, at least, the public perception of it is unfortunate, in that it appears to place far too much stress on the law of battery and a wholly inadequate stress on the doctors', nurses', and other professionals' duty of care. It is, of course, a draft code, and not, as some health authorities seem to think, a law enforced by the Secretary of State. We in the Medical Protection Society see – and I do not doubt that my colleagues at the Medical Defence Union perceive a similar trend – that the draft seems to instil fear in members of staff and persuades them to adopt a defensive attitude and practise defensive medicine.

As the last two speakers said, there is now a reluctance for doctors to act positively and clinically in the patient's best interests, and I think the reluctance stems largely if not entirely from the fear that they are going to be sued for battery. It would be encouraging if the publication of the proceedings of this meeting leads a move back towards encouraging professionals to pay greater attention to the law of negligence and their duty of care to the patients than to this defensive attitude towards avoiding possible accusations of battery. I think the balance is upset and needs to be redressed, and I certainly encourage those members of the profession who have asked me and my colleagues for advice to bear the above in mind and act in the patients' best interests.

DR MCGRATH: I should like to make two points. Firstly, I am very grateful indeed to Mrs Silberston for stressing that havoc can be created in a decent family by the presence of a badly affected schizophrenic person. In the days when I worked in general psychiatry before I went to work at Broadmoor, I had many examples of such families, and I interpreted the then law very liberally to secure the admission or readmission of such schizophrenic patients to hospital. There was a tendency, even before the 1959 Act, for consultants to discharge patients on a competitive basis. 'I have discharged more patients than you have. I am a better psychiatrist.' And this resulted in what the Italians call the *abandonnati* hanging around for example the railway stations – we have all seen them at Waterloo. We have seen them on visits to people's homes, wrecking the family milieu. I do not think this point could be too strongly emphasised.

My second point is that we have been, throughout, considering the level of ill- or well-informed consent purely cognitively. Can I illustrate, totally anecdotally, my slight difficulty in accepting this. A woman of robust physical and intellectual constitution suffered a subarachnoid haemorrhage. The pain made her distraught, to the extent that she would have given consent to any ill-informed advice. If anyone had told her that the amputation of her left ear and her right big toe would have relieved that pain, she would have signed her consent. Fortunately, of course, once again, we rely on the integrity and professionalism of doctors. She went into a highly prestigious neurosurgical unit and is now well. So perhaps we should look at pain as a factor in the giving of consent to ill-advised measures too readily.

DR SEYMOUR SPENCER: First of all, I congratulate Mrs Silberston on bringing common sense into the proceedings of this afternoon. I should like to consider one point. Mrs Silberston seems to be saying that the Schizophrenia Fellowship was pressing for what I take to be a community-treatment order; and she gave a number of reasons why guardianship was not being taken up, but left out the vital one which is the absurd subsection, whereby the person under guardianship can be taken to a place for treatment, but then not be made to accept the treatment when he or she gets there. This is an absurdity, as she points out. I would not have thought that a community-treatment order was necessary. All one has to do by way of legislation is to add to that subsection 'and receive treatment', and also add a clause so that a person on leave from hospital goes on receiving compulsorily the treatment he or she is getting. In my opinion, that particular change would cover the points that Mrs Silberston so rightly pleads.

MRS DOROTHY SILBERSTON: On the question of guardianship, we must look first of all at the period 1959–1983, and then post-1983. There was little or no take-up of guardianship, even though there were no problems about treatment, between 1959 and 1983. I suggest one will find that the real problems are the regulations governing guardianship. No right-thinking social-services department would assume guardianship for many such patients. There are a minimum of three monthly visits by a social worker to each such person stipulated, if they are in the care of the social-services department, apart from other aspects of the job. Similarly, not many social workers would take on such arduous tasks.

8 A response from the Mental Health Act Commissioners

SHIRLEY TURNER

I am very glad to contribute to the discussion as the official representative of the Commission, although other commissioners have spoken already. Indeed, David Sullivan was one of our most eminent members until his retirement in September. As I understand it, my role is to comment on issues that have been mentioned in other papers. I have not prepared a presentation, but am responding spontaneously to other participants.

The first thing that struck me in Dr Harris's paper, was that he chose the wrong bit of Wittgenstein. If I were going to quote this philosopher I think I should have chosen his ideas of areas of discourse. He developed theories about meanings depending on the way words were used in a particular setting by particular people. That is a gross simplification, but I think many of the difficulties that we are trying to resolve are due to different professions having different frames of reference. I think it was one of the lawyers who said 'The law is an ass', which is a very common term of abuse. I have been thinking along the lines that medicine is perhaps an ostrich, and philosophy is a skylark, not touching earth at all.

The Commission's view, in talking about the consent-to-treatment issues, has involved all these different areas of discourse. We perhaps have seen it in terms of concentric circles; in the centre, the doctor and the patient, the therapeutic dialogue, in some ways, a contractual situation; around them are the other professionals so closely involved in the very best psychiatric circumstances in their treatment and care, including social workers; round them are the families and friends who play such an important part in the patients' worlds and in the issue of consent to treatment; and round them is the law; and around all are ethics and morals, society's views on particular matters – not just philosophical approaches – but what ordinary 'people in the street' think. I have a great respect for Mrs Silberston, but I think that her 'man in the street' is certainly not 'my man in the street'. The sufferings of relatives of people who have been suffering from mental illness are so real to her and she puts them across in such a real way, that the views of other 'people in the street', including those of some patients themselves, were not represented in her discourse. I hope the Commission, with its lay members, represents these views.

I was pleased that Dr Murphy thought there had been a wide misinterpretation of the code of practice. Previous contributors have ascribed to the code of practice and our *Consent to Treatment* document what was not contained in them. So I hope we shall all go back and look rather more clearly at what really is in those documents.

I honestly do not think that the issue of battery will go away. Dr Mason, in helpfully giving the history of how the Act and the reference to the code of practice in the Act came about, said that perhaps the compilers should have looked less at the law of battery and now could move on to medical and ethical issues. But the law of battery is there, and it is there alongside the law of negligence. To quote from the *Consent to Treatment* document, in which our view is set out very clearly in section 10, we say:

> ''The law presents a conflict between the basic requirement of consent and the principle that a practitioner is under a duty to take reasonable care for his patient and to enable him to receive treatment which he needs. That conflict has not been resolved in relation to incapable patients.''

The purpose of the *Consent to Treatment* document was to try to set out this conflict and the arguments on each side, bearing in mind the law of battery, the law of negligence, and doctors' duties, all against the legal background and according to professional standards. I think that is quite clear. It has been suggested that the Mental Health Act Commission was anxious for patients to be detained, but section 10.2 sets out very clearly what the Commission feels are the four substantial limitations on the detaining of patients. In order to prevent the very large number of, for instance, 'elderly, severely mentally infirm and mentally handicapped' patients from coming, if they qualified, within the terms of detention and being subject to any attendant stigma that unfortunately lingers, we proposed that similar safeguards to those applied to compulsorily detained patients be applied to informal incompetent patients, without the latter being detained. I quote also from section 10.13, which deals with the issue of incompetent patients who refuse treatment.

> ''If there are difficulties in properly detaining . . . then good practice would require that the patient should not go untreated but should have as much protection as possible.''

The idea that the code and the *Consent to Treatment* document do not assist the professionals who wish to provide the care that the patient needs, seems to me such a gross distortion of what we were aiming to convey, that I find the misunderstanding very difficult to accept.

I wish to make other legal points. In my view, we have not got a rights-based legal system, as exists in the USA, in the sense of having a constitution, but the common law is based on principles, and one of those is of non-interference with the person, as we have heard. As such, there is not much distinction between the basic principles of our and American law; probably one of the reasons is that our system is much influenced by John Locke in the same way that the American system is. I do not agree with Mr Brooke in thinking that the principles governing conduct in everyday life or the argument relating to hostile touching help us very much in this area. Ian Kennedy joined David Sullivan in pointing out the tautology of this argument in one of our higher courts. As was said, there are other judgements that we can refer to, so I do not think we need to rely upon this latest Court of Appeal authority.[1]

I think it has been enormously important that we have been able to look at the subject of ethics. I have entirely accepted three-quarters of Dr Harris's argument. His idea of the respect for persons being a joint approach of concern for the welfare of the person and respect for their wishes, and his reference to John Stuart Mill, is very clearly incorporated in the intentions of the law and is very much the basis of the way we all look at our democratic society. I became confused when he went on to say that failure to treat incapable patients is a form of battery and the present law is nonsense. I suppose it is obvious that I would, for of course, battery is a physical touching. He presumably meant that the harm done in those circumstances means that failure to treat constitutes a metaphorical form of battery. And that may be so. But I think he and Mrs Silberston, and perhaps other speakers too, have side-stepped what for me is the most difficult issue: can you be sure that the health care that the professional wishes to give in the best interests of the patient is actually the most beneficial thing that can happen to that patient?

We in the Commission have thought about this problem a great deal in various aspects. I have been involved in looking at alternatives for what might amount to a community-treatment order. Mrs Silberston has mentioned this, and I am very glad to hear that the National Schizophrenia Fellowship is putting up a proposal as is the Commission. We have invited the Royal College of Psychiatrists and others to do the same. But there is a great deal of very sensible opposition to the idea of allowing professionals to require patients to have long-term medication against their will. The question of side-effects is the most obvious example. And to be sure that what we are doing is in the long-term interests of the patients is, I think, certainly not as easy as it seems.

Another problem, which came recently to my notice, was the idea of cosmetic surgery for children suffering from Down's syndrome. It has been

---

1. Mr Justice Wood, granting a declaration that termination of pregnancy and sterilisation of an adult woman incompetent to consent were not unlawful acts, was reported as having studied Collins *vs* Wilcock and Wilson *vs* Pringle (see p. 7), but "it did not appear to his Lordship that operative treatment fell within the phrase 'exigencies of everyday life'. The proposed operative procedures were *prima facie* acts of trespass" (*In re* T, 1987).

proposed that they would be more acceptable – I am not quite sure to whom – if their faces were more 'normal', and some surgery has been taking place. I have grave doubts about this treatment. Does it worry a Down's syndrome young woman that she has the features that go with the condition? Or does it worry those around her that she is so obviously a person who has a handicap? It is not an easy question. I think – because this is very important to somebody like me who is the parent of a daughter with a mental handicap – that the problem must be seen against the background of what happened in Germany in the 1930s, where some members of all professions colluded in experiments on, and the destruction of, people with a mental handicap.

So the Commission's solution, in my view, is not legal restraint. What we intended to do is to widen the area of professional responsibility. The development of exceptions to the rule that you cannot intervene requires involving the team, involving other doctors, involving a parent or a friend. None of these are easy issues, and I think there certainly are questions of whether one's relatives are one's best friends in these kinds of situations. I know that I, as a parent, am not always willing to give my daughter the autonomy that I think she needs in an ethical, legal, and medical sense.

We heard quoted both Popper and Martin Luther on putting primacy on private judgement, and Professor Murphy wondered whether there was merit in bringing three people's doubts together instead of one's. But I sincerely think that there is merit in the former, particularly if all three people are not of the same profession. I find enormous help in discussing difficult problems with other people. We have heard about the need to train doctors to look at ethical requirements, and I think they could also be trained both to retain their own sense of responsibility for their own professional approaches, and to work with others. And I am sure that is intended to be part of their training. But these requirements are difficult for all professionals, and lawyers are probably the most autonomous and non-co-operative people of all. The Commission had an example of the way professionals turn to ethical committees for guidance on questions of treatment. Staff at a mental-handicap hospital felt very much concerned, particularly with behaviour-modification programmes, as to whether they were going too far in interfering with the rights of incapable patients, and they formed an ethical committee that helps them discuss all such issues, not just research issues.

On the subject of research, Gordon Langley has already answered the question of whether or not we overstepped our remit. The reason we became involved in this issue – and it has caused us more problems than anything we could have imagined – is that we meant to be helpful. We did not give our sources because the draft code was not meant to be set out as a scientific document, being produced by a multidisciplinary group of all professions, but I think the sources of the information and the views expressed are very easily produced, and the chairman in a letter to the Royal College of Psychiatrists' *Bulletin* (Colville, 1986; *see also* Langley, 1986) has set out some of these.

I was very pleased that Sir Douglas Black referred to 'checks and balances' when he was pressed for an answer about research on the diabetic-coma patient, because the *Consent to Treatment* document sought to emphasise the need for balancing the importance of refusal or inability to consent against that of the need for treatment. Gordon Langley has mentioned what we took to be an acceptably broad definition of 'therapeutic' research, as put forward by the Medical Research Council. I was interested in Professor Jennett's sliding scale and his institutional review boards. The boards seem to be arriving at similar ideas to the ethical committees by a different route. I am pleased that Professor Jennett thought that the Commission's document had at least reminded doctors of broad ethical principles. The Commission intended only to set out principles it thought generally accepted, not to invent any of its own.

Dr Bewley's question concerned the hardest issue, that of the non-therapeutic, invasive research. As was said by David Sullivan earlier, there are areas in the research part of the document that very much need expansion and discussion. For example, might the powers of an attorney under the new Enduring Powers of Attorney Act (1985) be expanded to include the power to consent to invasive measures?

Mrs Teresa Myers said that there were similar supervisory bodies to ours in the USA but it was difficult to get the professionals to use them. I suppose that emphasises to me the importance of this kind of discussion. It is useless for anyone to set up bodies that might supervise or monitor if they are not going to be accepted by those who are undertaking the care of patients. So we need perhaps to benefit from the American experience and I would be interested to talk to her further about it.

I found Professor Murphy's practical examples extremely helpful. She obviously supports finding ways of putting morality into practice. I think she does accept that there need to be guide-lines in a way that Sir Douglas Black perhaps did not.

Professor Hirsch's idea of research relevant to patients of a particular class is a very interesting suggestion and maybe one that can be incorporated into the code. I had assumed that there was very much more agreement in the field on what were the categories into which research could be fitted so that agreed procedure at different levels of invasion or treatment could be set out. It is clear that this is not so and that people are coming forward with different ideas, but they do not seem to me to be contradictory. I hope that the research part of our document has stimulated the argument and brought all interested parties together.

In conclusion, I would like to emphasise once more what David Sullivan said, that we thought that the title *Consent to Treatment and Protection for the Incapable Patient: Legal Restraint or Professional Responsibility* for this symposium, most unfortunate; there is not an antithesis between legal restraint and professional responsibility, they are both part of the way our world should work when at its best. The *Consent to Treatment* document and the draft code of practice were both discussion documents and they have been successful in that they have promoted discussion. We are very pleased about this. Much of the detail that has been both praised and criticised arose because we were trying to answer questions that practitioners put to us. Strangely, the professional bodies had not produced such a document themselves. I think this is not because you do not believe that you need something; it is because of the very great difficulty of getting a sufficient consensus to put it forward. Now, I think partly as a result of the Commission's involvement in the area, all these questions are out in the open and they do produce a lot of anxiety, as Professor Murphy says. But surely it is important to deal with them. We all, as professionals, have to take part in this debate, and the contributors to this book are very well placed to do so.

I hope that everybody noted the emphasis given by both Mr Brooke and Mr Sullivan to their certainty that the courts would wish the professionals themselves to set the standards that would operate for consent to treatment for the incapable patient. The Commission put its documents forward as a genuine multidisciplinary effort. Each member respected each other's autonomy during the compilation and tried each to bring his or her professional best. And we hope that everybody here today will continue the discussion and that our work will not be wasted.

References

LORD COLVILLE (1986) The Mental Health Act 1983 draft code of practice. *Bulletin of the Royal College of Psychiatrists*, **10**, 220–222.
LANGLEY, G. E. (1986) A threat to psychiatric research? (letter). *British Medical Journal*, **293**, 133–134.

Cases cited

In re T: T *vs* T and Another. *The Times*, 11 July 1987.

Final discussion

PROFESSOR HIRSCH: Taking up the point made about the title of the conference, I think the nub of the issue is professional responsibility *vs* legal restraint, to take the extremes of the issue. In the past, we have relied perhaps too much on professional responsibility, allowing the consultant or GP complete authority to make the final decisions. There has been anxiety, in many cases quite reasonable, expressed about this when there were no 'checks or balances'. The Commissioners have tried their best, but their approach has been regulative and so tending towards the legislative. What is in the best interest of the patients in the long run? That depends to a large extent on how society works. A regulative society may have very clear laws of civil rights, and about the relationship between mental illness and restraint, as is reported in the Soviet Union, but the system may be misused. This probably occurred in Germany, even though she had a very good legal system. Then there is the society like Britain, with an informal but implicit code of conduct which – as I found out, as a newcomer 20-plus years ago – is by its nature difficult initially to grasp and establish for oneself. Such a system can work quite well in practice. Thus there is a contrast between, say, the American approach, which is deductive from a constitution, and the British approach, which one might say is developmental; each working similarly well in the respective countries.

Mrs Turner has described the attempt to regulate the British system, and Professors Jennett and Murphy, and Mrs Silberston among others expressed their reservations about whether this would result in the medical professions becoming very defensive in their practices. Although we all would like to think that the care of patients in the community is multidisciplinary, many patients would prefer that one, known, profession takes the final decisions in all cases. This could mean that social workers, for example, become the most prestigious caretakers in society – maybe those who would have become doctors and lawyers, would then be social workers instead! However, in British society today, I do not think that social workers take the same degree of responsibility for patients as physicians do, and they do not have anything similar to the doctor–patient relationship.

Although I recognise the need for more protection for patients with more safeguards than we have had in the past, I do not think this will be achieved by a regulatory approach. I suggest a 'half-way house' with guide-lines drafted broadly and in terms of how to achieve our established aims (I think this was Dr Harris's point) and with ethical committees etc. to allow for the flexibility and case-by-case decision-making which Sir Douglas and others have said is so important. The problem with regulation is that it results in the distancing of decision-making from those providing care, who consequently adopt a defensive attitude and transfer responsibility to the regulations.

PROFESSOR BRANDON: From the preceding discussion, it would seem that the man in the street operates in a world governed by the normal rules of conduct of everyday life and the lawyers act within a world subject to rules that they themselves have invented. Doctors, on the other hand, operate in a world in which the man in the street occasionally becomes so disordered that he ignores all the rules. When we have to cope with an immediate situation, we do not have time to consider rules in detail or to seek advice from others. Yesterday, in my unit, I had physically to restrain a lady who was about to leave, to put my arms round her as gently as I could and propel her back to the ward, because she was saying 'I want to go home, I want to go home.' I knew she was an agitated, severely depressed patient. My nursing staff and my registrar were so apprehensive about the interpretation of the rules that they were unwilling to detain her. They were not sure whether she was eligible for detention. She was not saying she was going out to kill herself, and yet, clearly, she was not fit to care for herself.

Considering matters from the patient's point of view, it is very easy to discuss in the cool logic of the committee room or the Houses of Parliament how we should formulate rules and how we should deal with them, but when we become ill it is a different matter. I – so far as I am aware, have not had a major psychiatric illness, but I recently had a major physical illness, and I found that all my views on consent, and how doctors should communicate were irrelevant – I just wanted them to get on with it and make me better!

DR JOHN BRADLEY: I am a psychiatrist and a member of the council of the Medical Protection Society, and in that capacity I have had the opportunity of examining over the last nine years some 60 or so consecutive cases of allegations of psychiatric negligence. It may be reassuring to some people to know that none has actually involved allegations of consent not being properly obtained, except for two cases of manic patients who objected to orders being used. Otherwise, of the 60 or so cases, half of them were of suicide or attempted suicide. Only two of those cases actually went to court and they were both informal – involving patients who had attempted suicide and injured themselves and who wanted compensation for not being restrained.

DR HARRIS: I want to take up one thing that Mrs Turner said. She was quite right to say that I side-stepped the issue of whether what the doctors proposed to do for people was in their long-term interests. I was assuming that treatment was beneficial, although there is every reason to be sceptical about the beneficial nature of all sorts of treatment offered to mental patients. I am just assuming that where it is clear that it is beneficial, then what I said, would apply, but I do not suppose that it always is beneficial. I am very much in favour of a healthy scepticism about the beneficial nature of treatment, but I was trying to identify a principle from a clear case. If I had talked for an hour rather than half an hour, I would have said a lot about the scientific status of much psychiatric treatment, but that is another issue.

MRS SILBERSTON: In relation to what the last speaker has said and also what Mrs Turner said in her closing remarks, I should like to know how the commission would establish whether our community-treatment order could or could not be to the benefit of patients. For how long would investigation be continued – considering patients will continue to suffer relapses in the mean time?

MRS SHIRLEY TURNER: What we are proposing is a development of guardianship. I shall not give all the details now. The Commission, by a majority, would wish to see a revised form of guardianship brought into effect very quickly indeed, firstly by producing a discussion document and making other professions and persons involved produce theirs. We shall then try to reach a consensus of opinion as quickly as possible, from all those who have views on the community-treatment order, from those who take the extreme civil-liberties side to those on the extreme 'Doctor knows best' side. Whether or not we shall be right or wrong, as you correctly say, can only be shown as we go along, but we want to get action in response to what at present we see as a need.

PROFESSOR JENNETT: I think the point raised by Dr Harris and earlier by Mrs Turner was the question: 'Is the treatment effective?'. We were all saying 'treatment' as though it was perfectly obvious that everybody knew what the treatment was and the only problem was to be allowed to give it. And, of course, research is partly about testing the effectiveness of treatment, which can only be done by proper trials, which involves asking for consent, some people being treated one way, some the other. That formal and effective scientific establishment of a treatment's efficacy is not done nearly enough, and yet there are almost no restraints on doctors treating people in exactly the way that comes into their head at the moment. I think we should have more research, and more formalised trials, which will mean more documents and more seeking of proper consent. We do not need nearly as much consent for giving casual treatment 'off the top of our heads' – this applies also to any branch of medicine.

DR A. R. M. FREEMAN: What Mrs Turner said has stimulated me in two ways. Firstly that the Royal College of Psychiatrists is currently putting forward a proposal for a community-treatment order. Without going into the details, it is based on modification of Section 3, Mental Health Act, rather than guardianship. Secondly, I felt Mrs Turner suggested that there was profound distrust within the Commission of the way doctors are likely to behave, which I think is a pity and, on the whole, this view is not shared by society as a whole. I would accept that there should be some way of regulating psychiatrists. What I still do not understand, from the lawyers' contributions, is why the Commission's chosen path has been through consideration of the law of battery rather than that of negligence. It seems to me quite acceptable that doctors should have clearer guidelines as to what is or is not negligent, because that does not interfere with the doctor/patient relationship. But overemphasis of the law of battery alters perspectives enormously, and causes the anxieties which have been mentioned, and it is most unsatisfactory.

MR BROOKE: I should like to follow up what has just been said because I have enormous sympathy with those people contributing to the discussion who are essentially concerned about care, and really very worried about the introduction of principles of the law of battery into their care for the patient. I hope that part of our exercise in this symposium is to build bridges between those of us who are trying to solve the problem with different insights. Of course, when one has got a patient who can consent and is coherent, then the elementary principles of the law of battery, that consent must be obtained before treatment is given, go without saying.

But we are dealing with people who by definition cannot consent because they do not understand, or those people who 'wander in and out through a half-world'; sometimes they understand a bit, sometimes they understand a lot, sometimes they do not understand anything. And I suggested that the interpretation of the law of battery by the judges, whether one has got the defence of consent or defence in other contexts, when people are touched, involves asking 'Is this acceptable?' We ought, being people who are seeing this problem from different insights, to evolve a solution in this difficult field to which the judges would say 'Yes, this is acceptable'. Mrs Turner stated that we must find 'exceptions', but I cannot see how a common-law judge can accept this. The Mental Health Act Commission has no legal power to make an exception; the Secretary of State has no legal power to make an exception.

DR BEWLEY: I wish to follow on from what Professor Brandon said. Perhaps we have not said enough about the issue of necessity; and I am reminded of something that Jonathan Swift said, which was that if a dangerous maniac were to enter this room today, we would knock him down and safely bind him first, then we would pity the poor creature. These first actions represent legal restraint under the heading of 'necessity', then pitying the poor creature is 'professional responsibility'; we would then think about what we could do for him.

I was very pleased that Mrs Turner said that the real purpose of issuing the draft code of practice was to stimulate discussion, because it has been very successful in that. I would have been much more worried if she had said that it was promulgating useful guide-lines. I think some of us have some reservations about it as it stands.

MRS TURNER: Referring to Dr Freeman's points, I am sad that you should think that I or any member of the commission has a distrust of doctors. Your very question seems to me quite extraordinary. It puts us in a 'them and us' position, which is quite false. Twenty-five of the 90 commissioners are consultant psychiatrists; we also have three GPs. Almost everybody has much contact with actual practice in the field. I think I have a healthy scepticism about all professions, and I believe very strongly in people acting together. But that does not mean to say I do not respect and acknowledge that there must be ultimate responsibility, and very often that is the doctor's. I should like to say again that we thought we were helping the doctor understand the framework within which he was required by the law to work, because I cannot accept the idea that the law is expendable, that you can put it on one side.

In response to Mr Brooke, I do not think that we as lawyers should be encouraging doctors to operate in ignorance of the law. We should support them to do what they feel is in the best interests of their patients according to the best standards of their profession. But I do not believe that we should be saying to them 'Don't worry about the law. Just get on with it.' I think we should be helping them to provide their own framework that the law can support in its natural development.

PROFESSOR MURPHY: They only comment I would like to make is that what has emerged today is the clear indication that the profession of psychiatry and the Royal College of Psychiatrists, and the Royal College of Physicians must develop its own guide-lines. Given what the Mental Health Commission is trying to impose on us, it is almost too late to have a total rethink, in terms of what the Mental Health Commission should be doing for patients. But it is sad that we should find ourselves in the middle of the 1980s in a position where we might be subject to many legal restraints in our treatment of patients. I think it is partly the fault of the profession that it has not produced its own ethical guide-lines. Perhaps it is not too late for us to do that, and I hope we can.

MR SULLIVAN: Mr Chairman, to reiterate, the law has developed piecemeal. The principle relating to battery is there and the law has recognised exceptions. In fact, in some of the cases you will find that general statements have been made by judges which are really to the effect that if they find circumstances in which they think that the action taken by, say, a doctor, or anyone else who makes contact with somebody else, was justifiable, then it is all right. It is retrospective law, as it were. It is that kind of principle that one can appeal to in saying that, given acceptable standards everywhere – and I mean accepted by society as well as by a particular profession – there will be justification held by the courts. That summarises my previous comments about courts recognising exceptions to the principle in relation to incapable patients if society establishes its own guide-lines – assuming the medical profession provides at least 85% of the input in drawing these up.

DR RHODE: That legal statement, representing a balanced view, is precisely what is misunderstood by the professions, resulting in them feeling that the primary consideration is the upholding of the law of battery, exceptions to this being of secondary importance. That is precisely why I got the response I did when I asked 17 social workers on a mental-health course last week what they would do in a real situation in which I had been the previous week. I was paying a very carefully prepared domiciliary visit at which the patient's family, doctor, and social worker were present. The professionals involved had known the patient for five years. As we met the patient at her door, she began to run away. In this circumstance, I and the others restrained and held her. We had an interesting interview in the garden, eventually she walked indoors and finally we committed her. I asked the social workers: In the event, would you have held her? Was it right? Or would you have let her go? And to a person they said 'let her go'. And I think this is because nobody understands what the law allows one to do.

DR BIRLEY: I should like to make a comment to Mrs Turner. If she went to Wisconsin, she would find a service by Professor Stein which I think has gained a lot of praise for community care, where patients are put on an order to the care of the service, not to the hospital, and it works very well.

Summing up by Dr Richard Nicholson
Deputy Director of the Institute of Medical Ethics

I am afraid that I am no Solomon, as somebody suggested I might be, and I feel that the proceedings have been reviewed very adequately by Mrs Turner. I think perhaps all I can do is leave you with what to me, as somebody who is not a psychiatrist but is interested and working in the field of medical ethics, were the main points made.

First I felt that the seriousness of the practical problems was not given enough emphasis, perhaps because there was not enough discussion of particular problems. For instance, the whole area that we have been discussing is one which has been of interest to me ever since I was a medical student. At that time, one of my friends in the settlement in the East End where I lived was a manic–depressive, and just this question of consent and incapacity arose when on one occasion he became manic and started trying to sell off all his property. I was able to prevent the bank manager and his solicitors from taking action until I had got him into hospital. I did this because he had said to me that he realised he was becoming manic and he wanted to go back into hospital. But when he got there he told the duty registrar that he was not interested in staying. Although the duty registrar knew him from the past, he told me 'Well, he doesn't want to stay, so I can't do anything. I know he's manic but that's it'. Finally, after he had ushered all the dossers from under Charing Cross arches into the National Liberal Club later that night, telling them that they would get a bed for the night there, and had then come back and done several thousand pounds' worth of damage locally in the East End, we managed to get the police to break the law, take him off private premises, and into hospital. So from the start of my medical student days I have been involved with the problem of what to do when somebody, just at the relevant moment, does not consent to what is obviously in his or her best interests. I was slightly sad that we did not discuss more of the really 'nitty-gritty', practical problems, because I think they are our main concern.

I was interested to hear of the law of battery being emphasised because, while I am sure that in psychiatric circles you may have been hearing rather too much about it recently, other doctors are all too little aware of some of the legal aspects of the work they do. I think in particular of a number of neonatal paediatricians I have come across recently, who look absolutely astounded if I suggest to them that there might be anything illegal about their undertaking research on the neonates in their care without either the consent of, or even the knowledge of the parents, and without bothering to tell the parents afterwards that they had done that research. So I think there are times when it is very important for all of us doctors to be reminded of the requirements of the law.

I was interested, again, in the emergence of debate on whether we want better training or better guide-lines. I think that in the long term, training is likely to be the answer, because I am fairly unconvinced of the value of guide-lines. I always look to the example of the very first guide-lines that were produced for the conduct of research, which were before the Nuremberg Code; they were produced in 1931 by the German Ministry of the Interior. It is an interesting reflection that a set of guide-lines produced in 1931, which are very similar in much of their content to the Helsinki Declaration, obviously had so little effect. Indeed, I think those guide-lines were the first formally written down to make the distinction between therapeutic and non-therapeutic research. I have the impression that there is a need for fairly prompt action on your, the professionals', part to establish the guidance you want. Otherwise, your avoidance of giving treatment etc. in difficult cases because of a state of indecision on these matters, may be accepted by the courts as the proper state of play. If professionals do not carry out the practices that count as exceptions to the law of battery, they might cease to be acceptable practices.

Research ethics committees were mentioned on several occasions. I certainly hope that what has been said about them at this meeting will apply a little more pressure on the Department of Health and Social Security (DHSS) to do what it should have been doing all along in monitoring whether or not these committees function adequately. The DHSS has only really taken an interest in research ethics committees on one occasion, putting out an advisory circular in 1975, and since then it has not in any way monitored what is happening in research ethics committees. They do not even have a list of the research ethics committees that exist in this country.

Finally, I think this meeting has been remarkably kind to the doctors, especially when one considers the activities of MIND and other organisations which led to the 1983 Act.

Index

compiled by **STANLEY THORLEY**

Date Due